AROUND THE WORLD IN 80 DISHES

Classic Recipes from the World's Favourite Chefs

DAVID LOFTUS

WITH A FOREWORD BY

JAMIE OLIVER

ATLANTIC BOOKS
London

First published in hardback in Great Britain in 2012 by Atlantic Books,
an imprint of Atlantic Books Ltd.

1 2 3 4 5 6 7 8 9

A CIP catalogue record for this book is available from the British Library.

ISBN: 978 184887 522 7

Designed by Smith & Gilmour, London
Printed in Great Britain

Atlantic Books
An Imprint of Atlantic Books Ltd
Ormond House
26–27 Boswell Street
London
WC1N 3JZ

www.atlantic-books.co.uk

'Monsieur is going to leave home?'

'Yes,' returned Phileas Fogg. 'We are going round the world.'

Passepartout opened wide his eyes, raised his eyebrows, held up his hands, and seemed about to collapse, so overcome was he with stupefied astonishment.

'Round the world!' he murmured.

'In eighty days,' responded Mr Fogg. 'So we haven't a moment to lose.'

Contents

INDIA

FRAGRANT SPICES 92

ASIA & THE ORIENT

AMERICA

THE ATLANTIC CROSSING

GREAT BRITAIN: THE END OF THE JOURNEY

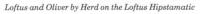
Loftus and Oliver by Herd on the Loftus Hipstamatic

A WELCOME FROM
JAMIE OLIVER

Welcome to *Around the World in 80 Dishes*. I've been hearing about this lovechild of Mr David Loftus for a number of years now and it's a complete pleasure not only to write this foreword, but to contribute recipes alongside all of these other incredible chefs. Every one of their contributions is a testament to David, who, if you think about it, probably knows a lot more about what's going on in food trends and publishing than most people. Because that's what he does. He works for anyone doing quality work and he travels to many, many countries to do it. A week can take him from east London to Jamaica to Chelsea to Paris and somehow he's made that work alongside being a wonderful father and husband, and a jolly good friend.

Around the World in 80 Dishes, to me, is Dave's excuse to instill in you a sense of place, to introduce you to knockout chefs, and to give you the real spirit of these beautiful dishes, and hopefully to inspire you to cook them yourself, regardless of where you live. It will pull you into another world. I quite like being simplistic about it: this book is like the Top of the Pops of exciting food – all of the best bits in one stunning volume. It is also a real celebration of David's temperament, personality and commitment – over nearly 25 years – to shooting food in a really honest, quick, no-nonsense way.

Let me tell you a little bit about David. He is quite a tender soul, he has a very relaxed, calm demeanor – he sometimes even rocks up to shoots in his pajamas with just one camera, one memory card and a couple of batteries (if you're lucky). And yet he's probably the fastest food photographer

I've ever worked with. As soon as something's put in front of him, its normally shot within 35 seconds or, at a push, a minute and a bit. And it's a pleasure because he always shoots with natural light, and the energy and spirit of each dish is always really honest and genuine. This might sound simple but, believe me, speed, honesty and being natural haven't been the standard in food photography for a long time.

I met David fairly early on – he shot my first-ever column with *The Times* magazine, a story about outdoor dining on the rooftops of London in St John's Street. I was running late and he didn't bring the selection of film he maybe should have, because he thought it was a daytime shoot. It was going on twilight, he shot on Tungsten film, and the honest truth is that I didn't see him all night. But when the column was published, all the plates of food looked amazing, there were people, wide shots, moving shots, macro detail, big location shots with the city skyline in the background, and I hadn't seen him once. I don't know where he had that camera but he must have been sticking it in places I hadn't seen – it was ninja, James Bond-style shooting. As soon as I saw the column I said, 'you've got to give me this man's number, he's a genius'. And from that day onwards I've worked with him on every book I've done.

Each book we've shot has had an incredibly different visual approach and I think that's one of the keys to being a great freelance photographer: being able to go from one job to another and take something unique and special to each client. Obviously this book is his baby, so this is David Loftus (aka Lord Loftus, descendant of Lord

Nelson) raw. And the pictures are simply outstanding, sweet, enchanting even. I remember someone doing a documentary about David once and I said on national television that he had 'a bit of a gay eye'. I definitely still stand by that. It translates in my mind as being able to find something beautiful and delicate within any dish from any country. And he totally gets that. I think it's probably fair to say that, technically, I know my way around his camera better than he does. David is not a big geek, to be honest; he doesn't even really like technology that much, although he uses it a lot. But what he genuinely does have is the incredible ability to take a beautiful picture. I've taken pictures of the same plate of food with the very same camera and still got nowhere near as good as the one that he effortlessly found a little angle for, or picked out a bit of detail in. I still find that fascinating because over the last fifteen years I've worked with many photographers. A lot of it is about kit, assistants, production and bravado, but I can assure you, there is none of that with

David – it's all about him, the camera and his genuine gift with photography. He doesn't exaggerate or big up his own work, in actual fact he's very humble and lets the pictures speak for themselves. Saying that, he does like to remind me every now and again that according to *Photographer Magazine* he is the 21st most important living photographer in the world (and I remind him that he's actually 65th, including his dead counterparts). As you can tell, he and I have really good banter, and that's what good work is all about.

But seriously, without question, he's one of the most prolific food photographers of the century. This book is David's dream and, as you can see from the choice of recipes and the stories written around them, the selection of chefs and the outrageously incredible pictures, it's a potent combination that I'm sure will look after many a wonderful meal with your friends and family for years to come. So often he's helping other people celebrate their books, and I'm really proud that this one is all about him.

Jamie Oliver

DAVID LOFTUS

My entire world revolves around food: on the road 350 days of the year, camera in hand, photographing the world's top chefs and their wonderful food everywhere from Battersea to New York to the Bahamas. I am in perpetual motion, it's usually summer, and I'm surrounded by the sights and sounds of a wonderful new country every week. Now, in *Around the World in 80 Dishes*, I want to share the most delicious food I have come across on my travels: eighty recipes by some of my very favourite chefs, many of whom are dear friends and who shared these adventures.

Some of the chefs' names will be familiar, others are rising stars, and some are culinary gods of the past. The best bread I have ever eaten was served to me warm for breakfast by the beloved, late Rose Gray of the River Café at the Tuscan home of chef Ruthie Rogers. I first tasted marinated rabbit barbecued on tiny wooden skewers by Jamie Oliver at the Petrolo Estate in Tuscany. Jamie served it with borlotti beans and greedy glugs of excellent extra virgin olive oil and we ate alfresco, toasting the sinking sun with a glass of lovely Galatrona wine. As I share my memories of an array of countries – and their food – and we cook our way through the gastronomic delights of those foreign shores, I hope you'll be transported by the tastes, smells and textures of these places and create some new foodie memories of your own.

I've loved tales of derring-do and discovery ever since I was a boy – perhaps that's why I've ended up roving the globe in the company of those who seek to create the perfect, mouthwatering dish, getting to the heart of a country via a plate of food and a little libation. But the story I loved best was Jules Verne's 1892 classic, *Around the World in 80 Days*. For not only is the novel's hero, Phileas Fogg, a courteous gent and global adventurer, he is also a meticulous foodie, nibbling, chewing and quaffing his way around the world. So, think of *Around the World in 80 Dishes* as a kind of culinary Baedeker – your guide on a Grand Tour that follows the route that Phileas Fogg set out to travel. And, as we circumnavigate the globe together, join me in meeting some of the world's finest chefs and hearing the tales that lie behind some of their signature dishes captured here.

If you love food and travel, and you've a hearty appetite for life, then I – alongside all the contributors whose copious passion, generosity and sheer genius bring these pages to life – hope that this book will inspire you to write, record, photograph and, of course, cook your own culinary journeys. So warm up the oven, pick a destination and prepare to set off…

Bon voyage, and bon appétit,

David Loftus

A. & N. AUXILIARY, C.S.
FRANCIS STREET
LONDON, S.W.

PAN   133

II

AH, leave the hills of Arcady,
Thy satyrs and their wanton play,
This modern world hath need of thee.

No nymph or Faun indeed have
For Faun and nymph are old and grey,
Ah, leave the hills of Arcady!

This is the land where liberty
Lit grave-browed Milton on his way,
This modern world hath need of thee!

A land of ancient chivalry
Where gentle Sidney saw the day,
Ah, leave the hills of Arcady!

LONDON: THE JOURNEY BEGINS

'Mr Phileas Fogg lived, in 1872, at No. 7, Savile Row, Burlington Gardens... He was one of the most noticeable members of the Reform Club, though he seemed always to avoid attracting attention; an enigmatical personage, about whom little was known, except that he was a polished man of the world.'

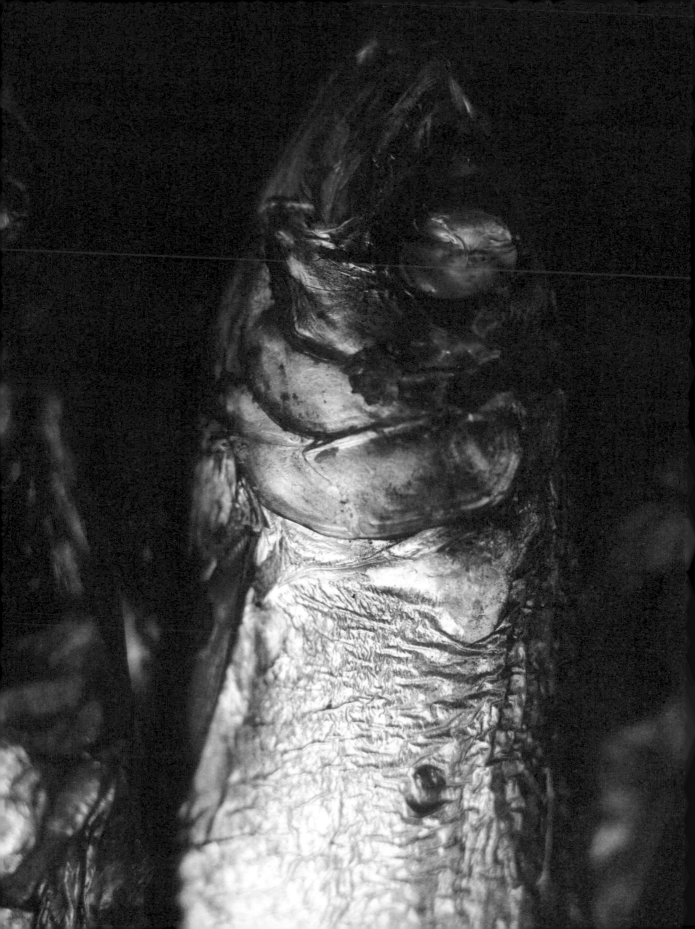

A REFORM CLUB BREAKFAST

Phileas Fogg's adventures begin on the morning of
2 October 1872 at his home in London's Savile Row.
Punctual, impeccably dressed, he sets out for a spot of
breakfast at the nearby Reform Club – a short walk that
he knows (having counted the metronomic click of his
shoe-heels along the same Pall Mall pavement twice a
day, every day, for many years) to be precisely 575 steps
with the right foot, and 576 steps with the left.

On his arrival at the club, Fogg assumes his usual seat
at his usual table – the one with the view on to the club's
courtyard garden – and awaits the three courses that
constitute the meal he eats each morning and each
evening for the entire season.

First comes a small piece of fish in 'Reading sauce',
a heady mixture of vinegar, sugar, peppercorns, onions,
brown gravy, gherkins, butter, salt, chopped tongue,
beetroot and hard-boiled eggs.

READING SAUCE: AN 'APPRECIATION'

Reading Sauce was the brainchild of fishmonger James Cock, who began trading from a shop on Butcher's Row in Reading in 1789. Bottled and sold to his customers, the condiment was intended as an accompaniment to preserved fish and had a deep, tangy, relishy flavour equivalent to something like Worcestershire sauce. The original family recipe called for 110 gallons of walnut ketchup, 25 gallons of mushroom ketchup, 12 gallons of Indian soy, 2½ gallons of chillies, 1 gallon of salt and a gallon of garlic. Remember this was pre-refrigeration, so one assumes the sauce was either very popular, or used often and very liberally, or both! The 1861 *Book of Household Management* includes a Reading sauce recipe that also calls for a fair volume of walnut pickle, shallots, Indian soy, ginger, mustard seed, cayenne – and one solitary anchovy.

Sybil Kapoor
GRILLED MACKEREL WITH GOOSEBERRY RELISH

Fogg may have been fastidious about his daily serving of boiled fish with sauce, but the very idea brings to mind a fair few school dinners my tastebuds would rather forget. Pallid plaice begone — catch of the day is Sybil Kapoor's recipe for succulent mackerel served with sweet, oozy gooseberry relish (which can be cooked well ahead and, if stored correctly, keeps for a good long time). Sybil is a modern-day Elizabeth David and I think Mrs David would have been excited by the idea of a dish that echoes the kitchens of Alexis Soyer at the Reform Club.

SERVES 4

4 medium-sized
  Mackerel, filleted
Olive oil
Salt and freshly ground
  black pepper
Lemon wedges, to serve

For the gooseberry relish
85g/3oz granulated sugar
1 small fresh chilli – red
  or green – seeded and
  finely diced
2.5cm/1 inch stick
  of cinnamon
3 black peppercorns
1 blade of mace
2 strips of lemon peel
1 tablespoon white
  wine vinegar
100ml/3½fl oz water
350g/12oz gooseberries

Put the sugar, chilli, spices, lemon peel, vinegar and water into a pan and place over a low heat until the sugar has dissolved. Bring the liquid to a gentle simmer for a few minutes, then add the gooseberries. Give them a good stir, then cover and leave to simmer for 6–8 minutes.

Using a slotted spoon, remove the gooseberries from the pan and place them in a clean bowl, leaving the spices in the syrup. Boil the liquid until it is thick and even more syrupy, then carefully pour it into the bowl with the gooseberries, removing the whole spices as you do so. Mix well and set aside to cool.

Preheat the grill to high and line your grill pan with foil. Place the mackerel fillets on a board, flesh side down, and with a sharp knife lightly make three evenly spaced slashes diagonally across the skin of each fillet. Brush each fillet with a little olive oil and season with salt and pepper.

Put the fish on your grill pan, skin side up, and place under the grill. As soon as the skins start to blister and turn golden, turn the fillets over and cook for a further 5 minutes.

Serve with lemon wedges and a generous spoonful of your gooseberry relish.

Alexis Soyer
MUSHROOM KETCHUP FOR A BLOOD-RED STEAK

Fogg continues his morning feast with 'a scarlet slice of roast beef garnished with mushrooms' and we're going to follow his lead with a mushroom ketchup from the Reform Club's Alexis Soyer. The word 'ketchup' comes from 'kôe-chiap' — used by Chinese seafarers as early as the seventeenth century to describe the brine of pickled fish — and the word sailed its way to our shores by way of maritime trading. The British used to pickle or ferment anchovies, oysters, walnuts or mushrooms for their ketchups and a splash of this fresh mushroom version on your blood-red steak makes for a zestfully spicy accompaniment.

MAKES ABOUT 3 X 450G/1LB JARS

700g/1½lb fresh dark-gilled mushrooms
1½ tablespoons pickling salt or table salt
25g/1oz dried porcini mushrooms
3 large shallots, peeled
1 clove of garlic, peeled
475ml/16fl oz white wine vinegar
10 allspice berries
4 whole cloves
3 blades of mace
2 bay leaves
½ teaspoon ground ginger
½ teaspoon freshly ground black pepper
4 tablespoons dry sherry

Begin by wiping your fresh mushrooms with a damp cloth and trimming off any dodgy ends. Slice the mushrooms thinly and put them into a ceramic bowl, along with the pickling salt. Give the mixture a good stir, then cover the bowl with a tea towel and set aside for the next 24 hours — occasionally giving it a few more stirs as and when you happen to drift by the kitchen.

An hour before you are ready to return to resume ketchup duty, you should attend to the dried porcini. Measure them out and place them in a bowl. Add 900ml/1½ pints of hot tap water and leave for about an hour, until completely soft.

Now you can start bringing the ingredients together. For this you will need a liquidizer or blender and a good heavy pan. First, remove the porcini from their bath, place them in the liquidizer, and purée until smooth. Put this mixture into your pan. Now transfer the sliced salty mushroom mixture to the liquidizer, blend until finely chopped and add to the pan along with the purée.

Next into the liquidizer go the shallots, garlic, and 175ml/6fl oz of the white wine vinegar. Again, give this a good whiz and add to the pan, then follow with the remaining vinegar, the allspice berries, cloves, mace, bay leaves, ginger and black pepper.

Place your pan on a medium heat and bring the contents to the boil. Then turn down the heat and simmer, uncovered, for about 1½ hours, or until the ketchup has thickened. Pass the mixture through a sieve to remove the spices and leaves, then put back into the liquidizer and blend until smooth.

Pour the ketchup back into the pan, add the dry sherry, and slowly bring to the boil, stirring constantly. When your ketchup is boiling, remove the pan from the heat and carefully pour the glistening sauce into clean pickling jars – remembering to leave a gap between the ketchup and the lid. Seal the jars tight, and plunge them into a bath of boiling water for about 20 minutes. Remove and cool the jars (and garnish with your own-brand labels). Superb with a slice of red-as-you-take-it steak, and a smooth glass of Barolo.

Tip: to cook the perfect steak – and Fogg specifies his to be 'scarlet' – you'll need one 3–4cm / 1¼–1½ inch thick beef fillet per person, preferably organic or free-range. It should be seasoned with salt and black pepper to taste, then patted with good olive oil, rather than oiling the pan. Place the fillet in a searing hot griddle pan for 2 minutes each side – a bit longer if you prefer your steak to be less rare than Fogg's. Squeeze on a little lemon juice, drizzle with extra olive oil, and serve with your mushroom ketchup. Pour the juices from the pan over the top.

David Loftus
RHUBARB AND GOOSEBERRY CHARLOTTE

Fogg chooses to conclude his rather lavish daily breakfast with a rhubarb and gooseberry tart served with a slice of Cheddar cheese. My great chum, fine fellow and blessed cheesemaker, Simon (farmer) Jones, makes a fabulous Lincolnshire Poacher. It's wonderfully hearty and earthy, just like its maker, who is so old fashioned and gentlemanly that he says hello to everyone he passes on a London street. This dish's combination of sweet, zingy flavours against the nutty crumb layers — and of course the tang of the cheese — makes for an extremely satisfying dessert.

SERVES 6 HEARTY CLUBBERS

450g/1lb mixed rhubarb, cut into chunks, and gooseberries
2 tablespoons brown sugar
25g/1oz butter, plus extra for the dish
175g/6oz fresh white breadcrumbs
A handful of finely crushed hazelnuts
¼ teaspoon grated nutmeg
1 teaspoon lemon juice
Seeds from 1 vanilla pod

To serve
A slice of Lincolnshire Poacher or Cheddar cheese per person

Preheat the oven to 180°C/350°F/gas mark 4.

Put the fruit into a large pan, add a little water and almost all the sugar, and cook gently until your fruit is soft enough to mush with a fork.

Butter a deep medium-sized pie dish (or experiment with individual portions). Scatter a layer of breadcrumbs over the base, along with a good sprinkling of crushed hazelnuts. Mix the nutmeg with the remaining breadcrumbs. Stir the lemon juice and vanilla seeds into the fruit. Fill the pie dish with alternate layers of fruit and crumbs, making sure to end with a layer of crumbs and the last of the crushed hazelnuts.

Finally, dot the top with butter and a final sprinkling of sugar, and bake in the oven for 25 minutes, or until the top is golden.

Serve each portion of charlotte with a slice of Lincolnshire Poacher cheese, which is widely available from delicatessens and farmers' markets. If you can't source the Poacher, you should go for a good, nutty, clean-tasting Cheddar.

THE WAGER

Having eaten breakfast in the style to which he is accustomed, all 'washed down with several cups of tea, for which the Reform is famous', Fogg turns to the day's papers. However, he is distracted from digesting both his food and the news by a conversation between friends. Emerging from behind his copy of the *Daily Telegraph*, Fogg joins his chums in their card-playing discussion of a recent robbery at the Bank of England. The British police are in pursuit of the well-dressed gentleman thief. Some of Fogg's associates speculate that because 'the world has grown smaller, since a man can now go round it ten times more quickly than a hundred years ago', the constabulary will have the edge on this shrewd fellow. Fogg agrees, speculating that since the opening of the Great Indian Peninsula Railway one might go around the entire world in just 'eighty days'.

The *Daily Telegraph* confirms the calculations:

FROM LONDON TO SUEZ VIA MONT CENIS AND BRINDISI, BY RAIL AND STEAMBOATS .... 7 DAYS

FROM SUEZ TO BOMBAY, BY STEAMER .... 13 DAYS

FROM BOMBAY TO CALCUTTA, BY RAIL .... 3 DAYS

FROM CALCUTTA TO HONG KONG, BY STEAMER .... 13 DAYS

FROM HONG KONG TO YOKOHAMA (JAPAN), BY STEAMER .... 6 DAYS

FROM YOKOHAMA TO SAN FRANCISCO, BY STEAMER .... 22 DAYS

FROM SAN FRANCISCO TO NEW YORK, BY RAIL .... 7 DAYS

FROM NEW YORK TO LONDON, BY STEAMER AND RAIL .... 9 DAYS

TOTAL .... 80 DAYS

Nevertheless, one incredulous gentleman remains unconvinced, maintaining that as a practical undertaking it would be quite impossible:

'Quite possible, on the contrary,' returned Mr Fogg.

'Well, make it, then!'

'The journey round the world in eighty days?'

'Yes.'

'I should like nothing better.'

And so Fogg makes his wager.

'I will bet twenty thousand pounds against anyone who wishes, that I will make the tour of the world in eighty days or less; in nineteen hundred and twenty hours, or a hundred and fifteen thousand two hundred minutes. Do you accept?'

'We accept,' replied Messrs Stuart, Fallentin, Sullivan, Flanagan, and Ralph, after consulting each other.

'Good,' said Mr Fogg. 'The train leaves for Dover at a quarter before nine. I will take it.'

'This very evening?' asked Stuart.

'This very evening,' returned Phileas Fogg.

EUROPE

'Passepartout mechanically set about making the preparations for departure. Around the world in eighty days! Was his master a fool? No. Was this a joke, then? They were going to Dover; good. To Calais; good again. After all, Passepartout, who had been away from France five years, would not be sorry to set foot on his native soil again. Perhaps they would go as far as Paris, and it would do his eyes good to see Paris once more.'

A PICNIC IN PARIS

Paris was made for picnicking – those *jardins*, those views,
and more to the point: those baguettes. For a rustic repast,
throw down a rug and spread out your wares.
My picnic-basket checklist goes something like this:

Chablis (chilled, and in a proper wine glass)
A morsel of something meaty, or perhaps the very special 'Conserve de Thon'
A cheese or two. Or more. One has to be 'Danyel's Filled Camembert'
Fresh crusty baguette
Salty butter (the best you can lay your hands on)
Fresh fruit, in season (some crispness, some squishiness)
A rug, a few napkins, the odd plate, assorted cutlery if it's going
Penknife (you'll never be sorry you packed one)

And whatever you do, don't forget the corkscrew.

Danyel Couet
CONSERVE DE THON
'TUNA IN A JAR'

Paris was made for a picnic and my Swedish Frenchman chum Danyel Couet came up with this 'tuna in a jar' recipe when working and romancing in the city. We once feasted upon a pot of this with a crusty loaf while sitting by the boating pond in the Jardin des Tuileries, a scene that can't have changed much in the last hundred years or so. Danyel serves his tuna with home-pickled olives, wine-cooked artichokes and his famous stuffed Camembert. Yum.

SERVES 4 PARISIAN PICNICKERS

400g/14oz ethically
  sourced fresh
  tuna fillet
Sea salt
2 lemons
2 cloves of garlic, crushed
4 sprigs of fresh thyme
2 bay leaves
1 teaspoon coarsely
  crushed black pepper
300–400ml/10–14fl oz
  olive oil

Slice the tuna into two equal-sized pieces and salt them well. Cover them with clingfilm and let them stand in a cool place for an hour. Peel the lemons with a speed-peeler, squeeze the juice and set the peel and juice aside.

After an hour, quickly rinse the fish and place each piece in a sterilized Kilner jar.

Distribute the lemon juice and lemon rind equally between the jars. Put the lids on the jars and put them into the fridge for about 3 hours, until the tuna has whitened.

Take out the jars, pop open the lids and add the garlic, thyme, bay leaves and black pepper, dividing the ingredients equally between the jars. Top up with olive oil, reseal the jars tightly and you're ready to picnic.

Danyel Couet
DANYEL'S FILLED CAMEMBERT

Danyel learned his trade at his grandmother's Parisian kitchen and is oft the provider of a fine picnic of tasty sausages from the Auvergne, slabs of sticky paté and stinky French cheeses. And so, all hail the Normandy village of Camembert and the cows that graze there, for without them and their cheese the picnic hamper would be a poorer place. Camembert is fabulous with fruit and particularly good served warm to accent the buttery, salty flavour at its creamy core. Lavished on a hunk of crusty bread, it's God's own gift to alfresco eating.

SERVES 2-4 HUNGRY PICNICKERS

1 ripe Camembert, chilled
1 dried fig, coarsely chopped
2 dried apricots, coarsely chopped
1 tablespoon sultanas
1 tablespoon currants
1 tablespoon chopped celery leaves

The key here is to think 'sandwich'. Imagine the Camembert round is a burger bun or any other sort of bread roll, and split it straight through the middle as you would if you were slicing open a bap. Mix the rest of the ingredients together in a bowl, and pack it all on to the lower half of the cheese as a filling. Pop the other half of the cheese back on top and press together well (just as you would press your palm down on to a good sandwich before munching). That's it. Easy as pips!

Wrap the cheese in greaseproof paper for your hamper. Eat it with a crusty baguette that you have daubed with expressionist strokes of salty butter.

Georgie Socratous
STRAWBERRIES AND BORAGE WITH FLAKED ALMONDS

I love borage. I've found it in almost all the countries I've visited, and I can never resist photographing it. When I pop my clogs I'd like borage to be grown on my grave. Grave-side borage. Traditionally a medicinal herb, it has long been used in Greek stews and soups or to fill pastas, but I hadn't eaten the little blue starflowers whole until I had them at the Crillon le Brave in the south of France, with strawberries and toasted almonds. It was stunningly simple and so good I had three portions. Borage is supposed to be mighty good for the tum… and for PMS.

SERVES 2-4

450g/1lb strawberries, hulled
A splash of Pimm's
50g/2oz flaked almonds
2 tablespoons icing sugar
A handful of borage flowers
1 teaspoon lavender
    flowers, dried

Preheat the oven to 180°C/350F/gas mark 4 and line a baking tray with greaseproof paper.

Cut the strawberries into halves and quarters, depending on size, and place them in a bowl. Add a good splash of Pimm's and leave to marinate.

Wash the flaked almonds in a sieve and drain them thoroughly, then put them into a bowl and toss with the icing sugar. Spread the almonds out on the prepared baking tray. Place them in the oven for 10–15 minutes. Repeat with the lavender flowers and add them to the baking tray of almonds once the nuts have been in the oven for 5 minutes. Remove once both are toasted and slightly golden. Let them cool.

Meanwhile, spoon the strawberries into a bowl and scatter over the borage. When the almonds are cool, crumble them over the top, sprinkle on the lavender flowers, drizzle with the leftover Pimm's from the bowl, and serve.

Rose Gray and Ruth Rogers
FOCACCIA WITH BLACK GRAPES

Fogg and Passepartout's journey from London towards Suez is undertaken at a clip, but a memorandum in Fogg's notebook confirms that their itinerary will take them through Paris and then on to Italy. This extraordinary bread was served to me warm for breakfast by the beloved, late, Rose Gray of the River Café at the Tuscan home of chef Ruthie Rogers. Possibly the best bread I've ever eaten, it was traditionally made to feed the grapepickers of Tuscany during harvest time, using some of the fruit that they had just gathered. It's so good we nibbled on it all day, until it was gone.

FEEDS 10...
FED 4 FOR A DAY

25g/1oz fresh yeast
200ml/7fl oz water
4 tablespoons sugar
8 tablespoons extra virgin
  olive oil, plus extra for
  greasing and drizzling
Sea salt
500g/1lb 2oz plain flour
1kg/2lb 2oz black grapes
4 tablespoons sugar
4 tablespoons fennel seeds

Dissolve the yeast in the water and add the sugar, olive oil and a pinch of salt. Put the flour in a mound on a wide clean work surface, and make a well in the middle. Add the yeast mixture, mix well, and knead for at least 15 minutes. Put the resulting dough into a bowl, cover with a cloth and leave to rise for at least an hour.

Preheat the oven to 180°C/350°F/gas mark 4 and grease a 30 x 40cm/12 x 16 inch baking tray with olive oil.

Take the dough, knock it back, and divide it into two. Press out one half of the dough on to the prepared baking tray as thinly as possible, making sure there are no holes. Spread with half the grapes, sprinkle with 2 tablespoons of sugar and 2 tablespoons of fennel seeds, and drizzle with olive oil. Press out the remaining dough and use it to cover the first half, crimping the edges and spreading the remaining grapes, sugar, and fennel seeds on top. Drizzle again with olive oil.

Bake in the oven for 45 minutes, or until brown and crisp. Allow to cool before serving, if you can resist.

David Loftus
SWEET TREATS FOR A SUMMER'S DAY

UNA FRAGOLA SURGELATA CON CIOCCOLATO

Jamie Oliver described me as a 'raving heathen' when I suggested this recipe to him,
but it is the only recipe I can claim to have given him, if you can call it a recipe. We were
toiling in the midday heat in the ancient and wood-fired kitchen of the Petrolo estate in Tuscany
when I went ahead, against his expert and foul-mouthed objections, and fed him beautifully
frozen fragola grapes from a height like an ancient Roman. Muscat grapes work really well,
but any grape will freeze. In the freezer, the juice inside turns to sorbet while the skin remains
hard and 'pops' to the bite. Jamie now serves his with hunks of chocolate and a nice chilled
glass of grappa, but I prefer mine with a glass of Petrolo's red.

APPLE TIMBALE WITH PINE NUTS

A dessert first tasted in a romantic canal-side restaurant in Venice and adapted
several times, this is a little different every time you make it, depending on your apples.
I remember that the chef toasted his pine nuts in the icing sugar but, done my way,
it is such a simple Venetian dish.

SERVES 4

2 apples
2 tablespoons pine nuts
1 tablespoon icing sugar
½ a lime or a handful
of pomegranate seeds
(optional)

Core your apples, then thinly slice or dice them into
matchsticks in the Venetian style. Carefully stack
the slices on a plate. Toast the pine nuts in a dry
frying pan on a low heat until golden, then scatter
the apple pieces with the pine nuts and icing sugar.

Squeeze over the lime juice, or scatter over some
pomegranate seeds.

Rose Gray and Ruth Rogers
THREE GREAT PASTAS

My favourite English Italians, Ruthie Rogers and the late Rose Gray, have led
me to so many gorgeous pastas, both in Italy and in England at the River Café.
I've loved them all, but these are my faves.

LINGUINE WITH BROAD BEANS

SERVED 4

3 tablespoons extra virgin olive oil, plus extra for drizzling
1 red onion, peeled and finely chopped
2 cloves of garlic, finely chopped
3 tablespoons chopped fresh flat-leaf parsley
Salt and freshly ground black pepper
2kg/4½lb broad beans (weight before podding)
350g/12oz linguine
60g/2½oz aged pecorino cheese, grated

Heat the extra virgin olive oil in a thick-bottomed pan, then add the onion and cook gently until soft. Add the garlic and half the parsley and continue to cook until the garlic has changed colour.

Season with salt and pepper, then add the podded or frozen broad beans and 100ml/3½fl oz of hot water. Cover the pan and simmer for 8 minutes. Drain off most of the excess liquid, leaving a little behind in the pan with the beans. Put half the beans, with their liquid, into a food processor and pulse-chop to a coarse purée, then put the mixture into a bowl and stir in the whole beans and the rest of the parsley.

Cook the pasta in boiling salted water until al dente. Drain, then add to the sauce, tossing so that the pasta is all coated. Stir in half the pecorino and drizzle with extra virgin olive oil. Serve with the remaining pecorino and a glass of very cold dry white wine.

FARFALLE WITH PROSCIUTTO, MINT AND PEAS

SERVES 4

100g/3½oz unsalted butter
200g/7oz large spring onions,
   trimmed and sliced
2 tablespoons chopped
   fresh mint leaves
500g/1lb 2oz peas
   (weight after shelling)
8 slices of prosciutto,
   4 torn into pieces,
   the rest kept whole
150ml/5fl oz double cream
Salt and freshly ground
   black pepper
350g/12oz farfalle
50g/2oz Parmesan
   cheese, grated
Extra virgin olive oil

Heat half the butter in a thick-bottomed pan, then add the spring onions and cook gently until soft. Add half the mint, together with the peas. Pour over enough water to just cover the peas and place the whole prosciutto slices in a layer on top. Simmer gently for 10 minutes, topping up if the water level drops below the peas.

Put half the peas and prosciutto into a food processor with the remaining mint and pulse-chop to a rough texture. Return the mixture to the pan and stir gently, then add the cream, bring to the boil and season with salt and pepper if necessary.

Cook the pasta in salted boiling water until al dente. Drain, retaining about 3 tablespoons of the pasta water, and add the pasta to the sauce, adding the reserved water if it's too thick. Serve with the torn prosciutto scattered over each plate, drizzle with olive oil and sprinkle with Parmesan.

TAGLIATELLE CARBONARA WITH PROSCIUTTO

SERVES 4

1 tablespoon extra
   virgin olive oil
300g/11oz prosciutto,
   cut into 1cm/½ inch
   wide strips
100g/3½oz unsalted butter
150ml/5fl oz white wine
6 egg yolks
50g/2oz Parmesan cheese,
   grated, plus extra
   for serving
50g/2oz aged pecorino
   cheese, grated
Salt and freshly ground
   black pepper
350g/12oz dried egg
   tagliatelle

Heat the olive oil in a thick-bottomed pan. Add two-thirds of the prosciutto and fry briefly, then add half the butter and all the wine. Simmer for 2–3 minutes.

Mix the egg yolks with the cheeses and season with salt and pepper. Cook the pasta in salted boiling water until al dente, then drain, reserving a few tablespoons of the pasta water to add if the sauce is too thick. Add the pasta to the prosciutto, then stir in the egg mixture, letting the heat of the pasta cook the egg. Stir in the remaining prosciutto and serve sprinkled with Parmesan.

Gennaro Contaldo
GENNARO'S PASTA & BEAN SOUP

Gennaro Contaldo: native of Minori on the Amalfi coast; fungi-finder general; curler of the most intricate and delicate pastas; as hospitable and generous as a man can be; and brewer of soups to warm the cockles of the hardest of hearts. Gennaro cooked me this soup when I was feeling particularly blue and it cheered me to the rafters. He served it on a tray next to a pile of beautifully wrapped antique tomes on 'world shipping'.

SERVES 6

500g/1lb 2oz dried borlotti
   beans, soaked overnight
   in cold water
8 tablespoons extra virgin
   olive oil, plus the bottle
   for drizzling
1 large onion, finely chopped
2 cloves of garlic, crushed
1 stick of celery, finely chopped
2 small carrots, finely chopped
100g/3½oz pancetta, finely
   chopped
1 large potato, finely chopped
1 bay leaf
3 fresh sage leaves
A few sprigs of fresh rosemary
A few sprigs of fresh thyme
A handful of fresh parsley
   stalks, finely chopped
2.5 litres/4¼ pints vegetable
   stock
200g/7oz pearl barley
Grated Parmesan cheese,
   to finish

Drain the soaked borlotti beans. Heat the olive oil in a large pan. Add the onion, garlic, celery, carrots and pancetta and cook until softened. Stir in the potato and herbs, then add the drained beans. Pour in the stock, bring to the boil, then reduce the heat to low and gently simmer for 1½ hours.

Rinse the pearl barley in a sieve, then drain and add to the pan. Continue to cook at a gentle simmer on a low heat for a further 1¼ hours. Check that the beans and barley are cooked before removing from the heat (if they're not, cook for longer).

When it's ready, serve the soup ladled into bowls, with a drizzle of good extra virgin olive oil and a sprinkling of Parmesan for an extra rich hit.

num, fi L cta qualicaribus vini ef-
fet in certa : non igitur eft di-
inde Tridentinum fef-
Canone fecundo

ria confecrationis, & vinum album,
vel nigrum, fiquidem unum é duo-
bus necessario electum fuit. Sed il-
lud eft Sacrameto necessarium, quod
ad veritatem formæ necessari
fuerit, quodque Chriftus D
pro Sacramento confe

christiani fimi. Capite aurem feptima
hæc leguntur: [Mulier quædam di-
vino amore inflammata, pia quidem
mulier, & fructibus ipfis pietatem
demonftrans, Sanctum rogat, utin
ipfius domeftico facello facram of-
ferat Liturgiam. Ecce autem mira-
culum omnibus, quotquot unquam
acciderunt miracula exequandum.
Ubi mulieris fides, ibi divina cele-
brantur.*a*) miracula, ubi verò ira
ndia, femper malitia aliqua erum
U traque in uno Prophetæ
quetur, in folitudin
Eíias, cùm ipfum J
tribilis ille Prophet
acerdores comba
usfit, & ficcitat
dua Sareptæ
noe filium,
evocar
müli
fat

[*a*] *Haec mistio*
eft ex præcepto
Ecclesiæ.
(*b*) Sic Vasó
diu. 17. cp.
z. Suar. cîm
47. fch. z. Æ
gid. de Coïm
ch. quaft. 74.
art. 5. n. 15.
Benac. disp. 4.
9. q. a. p. 8.

juftum cor ai
falfum eft, 8
Cypriano dice
us off, fan
fic fi nobis]
quod fig ficet unic
cum Chrifto; fed eft
ur ficu: farina fola,
non poteft licitè nec
ri, quia nec farina
fola eft panis; fic nec
licitè poteft confecrar
lide poffit, quia folu
aqua eft verum, imò r
vinum : uti Ulrico Pres
git, qui aquam forte no.
nihilomini, confecravit,
miraculo ap   Adve
dò, (*b*) huj   tion
ex præcepto
Ecclefiaftico en
veorex Tridentin
dicentibus, ex Eccle
hanc mixtionem haberi,
indicarunt non ex Chrifti intu.
ne. Nam efto Ecclefia præcipe
poffit obfervandum idipfum, quod
Chriftus præcepit, incongruè tamen
judicarent ab ea obligationem oriri,
cùm præcipua obligatio ex Chrifti

[*c*] Explican
tur Concilia, &
Paute.

effe offerend
Chriftus
pag

ac
quam præ
tum præmi
nquam fecund
pro noftrâ falute
ratione, ac fufpenfione eft
firicerit, farig usfit. Mulier eûdem
à forore inculata, audirex ipfo ver
to, bonam partem elegiffe, quæ in

lego corpori
Fecrationis mater
Arfi aqua
certius III. C
ma Trinitate, expr
(*a*) Dicta verò

vi
gis Chri

unum effe, in Sacrificio nihil aliud   diarè convertetur, n

EGYPT AND THE MIDDLE EAST

'Little by little the scene on the quay became more animated; sailors of various nations, merchants, ship-brokers, porters, fellahs, bustled to and fro as if the steamer were immediately expected. The weather was clear, and slightly chilly. The minarets of the town loomed above the houses in the pale rays of the sun. A jetty pier, some two thousand yards along, extended into the roadstead. A number of fishing-smacks and coasting boats, some retaining the fantastic fashion of ancient galleys, were discernible on the Red Sea.'

THE STEAMSHIP MONGOLIA

'The steamer *Mongolia*, belonging to the
Peninsular and Oriental Company, built
of iron, of two thousand eight hundred tons
burden, and five hundred horse-power, was
due at eleven o'clock a.m. on Wednesday, the
9th of October, at Suez. The *Mongolia* plied
regularly between Brindisi and Bombay via
the Suez Canal, and was one of the fastest
steamers belonging to the company, always
making more than ten knots an hour
between Brindisi and Suez, and nine and
a half between Suez and Bombay.'

Andy Harris
EGYPTIAN LENTIL SOUP

Fogg's journey continues on towards Port Said and the mouth of the Suez Canal aboard the steamship *Mongolia*. I imagine Fogg on a cold October day, with the coast of Egypt in sight, warming his hands with a steaming bowl of soup as he looks over to the minarets on the shore, which 'loomed above the houses in the pale rays of the sun'. I was sitting aboard the ancient *Thelginos*, sailing a sunset sea to Mount Athos, when Andy (of Arabia) Harris first fed me this delicious soup. The next time I supped on it I was watching dhows leave a Bahrain seaport in the late evening mists on their way to their shrimp catch.

SERVES 4 GENEROUS PORTIONS

2 teaspoons butter
2 carrots, chopped
2 cloves of garlic, crushed
2 sticks of celery, chopped
2 onions, chopped
1 bay leaf
1 large tomato, chopped
1 teaspoon ground cumin
½ teaspoon ground coriander
475ml/16fl oz chicken stock
200g/7oz dried red lentils, washed and checked for stones
475ml/16fl oz water
Salt and freshly ground black pepper

For the caramelized onions
4 or 5 onions, cut into small wedges
Salt
Balsamic vinegar (optional)
Fresh thyme leaves (optional)

Melt the butter in a large pan and add the carrots, garlic, celery, onions and bay leaf. Cook gently on a medium heat until the onions are soft and golden.

When the vegetables are tender, add the tomato, spices, chicken stock and lentils. Pour in the water, bring to a gentle simmer, cover the pan with a lid and leave for about 30–40 minutes, until the lentils are soft. Take the pan off the heat.

For a smooth soup, you should give it a good whiz in a blender. If you prefer more texture, just give the ingredients a gentle mash with a fork. If you do choose to blend, pour the soup back into the pan when smooth. Either way, bring it back to the boil, add salt and pepper to taste, and heat thoroughly for a few minutes, stirring constantly.

Serve topped with a small hill of caramelized onions. Onions are naturally sweet, and easily melt down to a sticky caramelization. Just throw the onion wedges into a pan with a pinch of salt, and cook on a medium heat until they turn a glistening golden brown. Serve them as they are, or try adding a splash of balsamic and a sprinkling of fresh thyme leaves at the end. Either way, the onions are a yummy garnish for a yummy soup.

Andy Harris
CLASSIC FUL MEDAMES

The Suez Canal opened in 1869 and in one fell swoop reduced the journey to India by half — the arduous half, in fact, since there was no longer any need to travel via the Cape of Good Hope. While the *Mongolia* is in dock, and her crew prepare for the onward journey to Aden (some 1,310 nautical miles), Fogg remains in his cabin and waits to be served. My favourite Egyptian dish is ful medames, again introduced to me by Andy Harris. Very simple, very ancient, and vastly popular, it is made with slow-cooked dried fava beans and is traditionally eaten at breakfast, though it's filling enough for lunch or supper.

SERVES 4

700g/1½lb dried fava
  beans or dried broad
  beans, soaked overnight
  in cold water
2 cloves of garlic, crushed
1 tablespoon lemon juice
55ml/2fl oz extra virgin
  olive oil
½ teaspoon ground cumin
Salt and freshly ground
  black pepper

To serve
1 fresh egg per person, boiled
Extra virgin olive oil
½ red onion, finely sliced
1 tablespoon flat leaf parsley,
  finely chopped
Flatbreads, gently warmed
  through

Drain the beans and put them into a large pan. Cover with fresh cold water, bring to the boil and simmer on low heat for about 1 hour.

Drain the beans again, and discard the cooking liquid. Place your cooked beans in a bowl, add the garlic, lemon juice, olive oil and cumin and combine well. Season with salt and pepper if it needs it, and serve each portion topped with a boiled egg, a drizzle of good extra virgin olive oil, and garnished with the red onion and parsley. Egyptians commonly mash everything together with a fork or a spoon and use flatbread as a scoop for eating.

Debbie Loftus
FRESH FIGS WITH HOT ESPRESSO SYRUP

To reach Aden, in the Yemen, Fogg and Passepartout sail the length of the Red Sea, past the city of Mocha and its 'vast coffee-fields', then through the Strait of Bab-el-Mandeb — the 'Bridge of Tears'. The journey is unpredictable and rough, but Fogg still takes 'his four hearty meals every day, regardless of the most persistent rolling or pitching on the part of the steamer'. This recipe, introduced to me by my wife and rock cake Debbie on a rooftop in Marrakesh, combines beautiful Arabica coffee, rich fleshy fruit, and a sweet-and-spice hint of things to come…

SERVES 4

8 fresh figs, halved
75g/3oz soft brown sugar
250ml/8fl oz strong
  Arabica coffee
A pinch of ground
  cinnamon
1 star anise
Vanilla ice cream,
  to serve

Put the figs into a bowl. Place the sugar, coffee, cinnamon and star anise into a small heavy-bottomed pan (preferably a stovetop coffee pan, of the kind used to make Turkish coffee). Bring to the boil, and continue to boil until you have a thick syrup to pour straight over the figs. Serve with a scoop of good vanilla ice cream.

Debbie Loftus
DATE AND COFFEE LOAF

Debbie only makes breads that are really special, believing that one should buy a baker's bread and not try to make it for oneself! She is also an artist, so the aesthetics of the loaf are very important to her. This is a particularly beautiful, dark and rustic-looking sweet bread that wouldn't be easy to find at your local bakery. It smells and tastes amazing, and it is hard not to consume the whole loaf in one sitting – especially if it's warm and covered in melted butter.

SERVES 8-10

250g/9oz pitted dates, chopped
1 teaspoon bicarbonate of soda
250ml/8fl oz strong Arabica
  coffee
2 tablespoons softened butter
2 tablespoons white sugar
1 free-range egg, beaten
1 teaspoon vanilla extract
150g/5oz plain flour
1 teaspoon salt
150g/5oz pecan nuts, chopped

Preheat your oven to 180°C/350°F/gas mark 4. Grease a 20 x 10cm/8 × 4 inch loaf tin and line the bottom with baking parchment.

Put the chopped dates into a bowl and sprinkle with the bicarbonate of soda. Bring the coffee to the boil in a small pan and pour over the dates, then set the bowl aside.

In another bowl, vigorously mix the butter, sugar and egg until well blended – either by hand or with a hand-held electric whisk. Using a metal spoon, blend in the vanilla extract. Add the flour and salt and gently blend, then finally fold in the chopped pecan nuts and the date and coffee mixture. Pour into the prepared loaf tin.

Place in the centre of the oven and bake for approximately 1 hour, or until the top of the loaf springs back when lightly pressed. When the cake is ready, let it stand for a few minutes before removing from the tin, peeling off the baking parchment and leaving to cool on a wire rack.

Try serving a slice with a weak Yemeni coffee, sweetened with a little sugar and preserved ginger.

Nigella Lawson
OVERNIGHT LAMB SHANKS WITH FIGS AND HONEY

Aden, on the Yemeni coast, is the *Mongolia*'s final port of call before Fogg sets sail for India. Verne calls it 'the Gibraltar of the Indian Ocean' and like Gibraltar, Aden acts as a kind of gateway between two cultures — Arabia and India — and the influence of both is discernible in this dish. Sweet and aromatic, like Nigella, these lamb shanks create the most delicious smell and taste just as good.

SERVES 10

4 tablespoons olive oil
10 lamb shanks
1kg/2lb 2oz onions, finely chopped
2 cloves of garlic, finely chopped
Leaves from 4 sprigs of fresh thyme or 2 sprigs of fresh rosemary, finely chopped
1 x 425g tin of pumpkin purée
450g/1lb dried figs
1 teaspoon ground allspice
2 cinnamon sticks, broken up
75ml/3fl oz runny honey
1 bottle of red wine
500ml/17fl oz water
Salt and freshly ground black pepper

You'll need a very large pan for this very large stew. First, heat the oil in your pan and brown the shanks in batches. Set them aside. Add the onions, garlic and herbs and fry them gently in the oily pan until the onion is soft, not coloured.

Add the pumpkin purée, figs, allspice, cinnamon sticks, honey, wine and water. Stir well and bring to the boil. Put the shanks into the boiling liquid, turn down the heat and simmer for 1½ hours, partially covered.

Pop the pan on a window-sill, or somewhere cool, and leave until cold. Use a slice or spoon or even your hands to remove the layer of fat that will have formed over the surface of the stew.

The following day, reheat the stew gently and check the seasoning, adding salt and pepper as necessary. Serve with rice cooked with turmeric and sprinkled, on serving, with pomegranate seeds.

David Loftus
CHICKEN TAGINE
WITH LEMON AND OLIVES

The delicate spices and jewelled fruitiness prevalent in Arabic food beautifully combine with the more fiery, tangy flavours of Indian influence in this classic tagine. I've had some fabulous tagines in the belly-dancing bars of North Africa, but my favourites are the simpler versions created by the cooks, Aicha and Sophia, at my friend's riad in Marrakesh. If I close my eyes, this dish sends me straight back to their jasmine-scented home in the heart of the medina.

MAKES 8 HEARTY PORTIONS

1.8kg/4lb chicken thighs
   and legs
2 teaspoons paprika
1 teaspoon ground cumin
1 teaspoon ground ginger
1 teaspoon ground turmeric
½ teaspoon ground cinnamon
½ teaspoon freshly ground
   black pepper
Olive oil
A pinch of salt
4 cloves of garlic, mashed
1 onion, finely chopped
Thin slices of rind cut from
   1 preserved lemon
150g/5oz pitted green olives
60g/2½oz raisins
120ml/4fl oz water
3 tablespoons chopped
   fresh coriander
1½ tablespoons chopped
   fresh parsley

Pat the chicken pieces dry. Place them in a large bowl and sprinkle with the spices. Roll up your sleeves and use your hands to make sure the meat is well coated. Set aside for an hour.

When ready to cook the chicken, pour a few glugs of olive oil into a large, heavy-bottomed pan. Heat the oil on a medium heat and add the chicken pieces. Brown gently, adding a little salt. Then lower the heat, add the garlic and onions, cover the pan and let it all gently cook together for 15 minutes.

Now open the lid and turn the chicken pieces over. Add the preserved lemon rind, olives, raisins and water. Bring to a simmer, then take the heat down to a low setting again, cover the pan and cook for about 30 minutes, until the chicken is tender and cooked all the way through.

Stir in the fresh coriander and parsley and serve with nice plain couscous and a bowl of yoghurt. Delicious.

Jamie Oliver
JAMIE'S SEAFOOD RISOTTO

The final leg of this long journey by steamship will take us across the Arabian Sea. Let's bid farewell to the Middle East with a very special ingredient that is also found in Indian cooking: saffron. The bulb is said to have first made its way to England in the pocket of a son of Essex who found it in Tripoli. The flower adapted nicely and grew very well in the fields around our pilgrim's home – so much so that the area became known as Saffron Walden ('walde' being the Anglo-Saxon for 'field'). When I asked Jamie Oliver for his favourite saffron-based recipe, he shouted, 'Lord of Loftus, it is the seafood risotto I made for you on the steps of Villa Petrolo, don't you remember?' I do...

SERVES 6

1.1 litres/2 pints organic
   fish stock
2 tablespoons olive oil
A knob of butter
1 large onion, finely chopped
2 cloves of garlic, finely
   chopped
½ a head of celery, finely
   chopped
½ a bulb of fennel, finely
   chopped, herby tops reserved
1 teaspoon fennel seeds
A pinch of crumbled dried chilli
A pinch of saffron strands
400g/14oz risotto rice
2 wine glasses of dry white
   vermouth or dry white wine
Sea salt and freshly ground
   black pepper
1.5kg/3½lb cleaned and
   prepared mixed seafood

To finish the risotto
70g butter
Extra virgin olive oil
Juice of 1 lemon
Leaves from a small bunch
   of fresh parsley, chopped

Red mullet, monkfish, bream, John Dory, cod, mussels, clams, prawns and squid would all be suitable for this recipe. Put a shallow pan on a medium heat and fill three quarters of the way up with boiling water. Poach the fish, excluding any squid, prawns or shellfish, for 3–5 minutes, or until cooked through. Leave to cool a little while you get on with the risotto.

Heat the fish stock in a large pan. Put the olive oil and butter into a separate pan, add the onion, garlic, celery, fennel, fennel seeds, chilli and saffron and cook slowly for 15 minutes without colouring. Add the rice and turn up the heat. Stir for a minute, then add the vermouth or wine.

Now add a ladleful of the hot stock and a pinch of salt. Turn down to a simmer and keep adding ladlefuls of stock, stirring and letting each one be absorbed before adding the next. After about 15 minutes the rice should be soft but still have a slight bite. Flake the fish into the risotto and add any squid, prawns or shellfish – after 3 or 4 minutes the shellfish will have opened (discard any that remain closed). Remove the pan from the heat.

Add the butter, and season with salt and pepper. Drizzle with extra virgin olive oil and squeeze over the lemon juice. Serve sprinkled with the parsley and the reserved fennel tops.

INDIA

'On Sunday, October 20th, towards noon,
they came in sight of the Indian coast...'

BOMBAY TO CALCUTTA:
A LONG JOURNEY BY TRAIN
(AND ELEPHANT)

'The locomotive, guided by an English
engineer and fed with English coal, threw
out its smoke upon cotton, coffee, nutmeg,
clove and pepper plantations… They came
upon vast tracts extending to the horizon,
with jungles inhabited by snakes and tigers,
which fled at the noise of the train; succeeded
by forests penetrated by the railway, and still
haunted by elephants which, with pensive
eyes, gazed at the train as it passed.'

Dr Loftus and Danyel Couet
INDIAN CHUTNEY AND PICKLE

Fogg and Passepartout embark on a long train journey, heading east from Bombay to Calcutta: the Great Indian Peninsula Railway has arrived. Train journeys require a plentiful supply of snacks to keep the hunger-pangs to a minimum and stave off the dreaded boredom. My father used to say, 'No meal is complete without cheese.' And in India the same might be said of chutney and pickle: whether for a snack or a main course, it's the chutney and pickles that make the meal. Here are recipes for a gorgeous tomato chutney and a peach pickle to accompany any savoury nibbles you might encounter.

DR LOFTUS'S SWEET AND SPICY TOMATO CHUTNEY

MAKES 4–5 LARGE JARS
600ml/1 pint malt vinegar
1kg/2lb 2oz ripe tomatoes, chopped
500g/1lb 2oz onions, quite finely chopped
3 cloves of garlic, finely chopped
2 eating apples, peeled, cored and chopped
2 teaspoons mustard seeds
2 cloves
A thumb-sized piece of fresh ginger, peeled and grated
300g/11oz sultanas
200g/7oz light muscovado sugar
Salt and freshly ground black pepper

Put half the vinegar and all the other ingredients into a large deep pan. Bring the contents to a simmer over a medium heat, and stir constantly until the sugar has dissolved.

Keep the pan on the heat and leave the chutney to cook for about 40 minutes, stirring every now and then. When the time is up, stir in the rest of the vinegar and continue to cook for a further 30–40 minutes, stirring regularly until thickened.

Divide the chutney between sterilized jars and set aside to cool. When cooled, place a disc of waxed paper over the chutney and seal with an airtight lid or cellophane – either way, make sure the seal is good. Store in a cool dark place for a month before eating, after which time it is ready for you to enjoy with whatever snack or meal you fancy.

DANYEL COUET'S PICKLES À LA PÊCHE

Danyel's peach of a pickle is a picnic pickle to be proud of. It was inspired by his wanderings around the Indian markets and restaurants of Northern Paris as a culinary student in search of new ideas beyond the bistros and fine dining rooms of the city.

MAKES 3–4 LARGE JARS

2 shallots, finely sliced
4 tablespoons apple cider
   vinegar
2 tablespoons fennel seeds
1 stick of cinnamon
2 tablespoons anise seeds
¾ of a tin of chickpeas, drained
165g/5½oz currants
3 fresh red chillies, chopped
1 tablespoon grated fresh
   ginger
450g/1lb Demerara sugar
600ml/1 pint cider vinegar
Sea salt
900g/2lb ripe peaches, stones
   removed, flesh cut into
   segments
3 teaspoons chopped mint

Put the shallots into a bowl with the apple cider vinegar and set aside.

Roast the fennel seeds, cinnamon and anise seeds in a hot dry pan. Except for the peaches, mint and shallots in vinegar, put all the ingredients into a large pan. Simmer on a low heat for 10 minutes, then set aside and leave to cool.

Add the peaches, mint and shallots in vinegar to the pan and stir gently. Transfer to sterilized jars, seal with tight-fitting lids and store in a cool place. Serve as a snack, with poppadoms.

Jamie Oliver
JUNGLE RABBIT TWO WAYS

I've never been a great fan of rabbit. Thoughts of fluffy bunnies get in the way, but I shouldn't be so sentimental. Rabbit meat is very healthy, tastes incredible, and your local butcher will happily chop it into thighs and leg, belly and saddle, liver and kidney. Jamie Oliver has cooked me some delicious rabbit dishes – rabbit in risotto, rabbit on toast – but my favourite by far is a marinated rabbit barbecued on tiny wooden skewers. He first made it for me one evening with borlotti beans and glugs of extra virgin olive oil. We ate alfresco and toasted the sinking sun with a glass of lovely Galatrona wine.

JAMIE'S ITALIAN MARINADE FOR RABBIT

To make enough marinade for one rabbit (or chicken), jointed, put a small bunch of fresh thyme and a small bunch of fresh rosemary into a mortar. Add a couple of cloves of garlic and the zest and juice of a lemon, plus a good lug of extra virgin olive oil. Mix, bash and crush to a fragrant pulp, then pour it over your bowl of rabbit pieces and rub it well into the meat. Marinate for an hour, then skewer and barbecue if you can – or roast in the oven, if not – constantly turning and brushing with the marinade.

The joints cook at different speeds. Do the legs and shoulder first, add the belly 10 minutes later, then the saddle and ribs 10 minutes after that. Last but not least, pop in the kidneys and liver with some lovely pancetta.

Serve with some white beans and good olive oil.

JAMIE'S CLASSIC TIKKA MARINADE

For a rabbit snack that's more Bombay Central Station than Grand Centrale Roma, Jamie suggests smothering the meat in a classic tikka marinade. Again, this makes enough for one rabbit (or chicken), jointed.

Mix together 6 tablespoons of yoghurt, the juice of a lemon, a 2.5cm/1 inch cube of fresh ginger, grated, 3 cloves of garlic, peeled and grated, a teaspoon each of ground cumin and salt, and ¼ teaspoon each of garam masala, turmeric and cayenne pepper. Slather the mixture over your rabbit pieces and marinate for an hour or longer – leave overnight for a more potent mix!

Thread it on to wooden skewers (remembering to soak them in water beforehand) and barbecue till crisp and tender. Serve on a bed of rice.

Dr Loftus
MASOOR DHAL

At Burhampoor, under the midday sun, our heroes purchase a hasty lunch (and some rather fine Indian slippers) from the platform before heading back to the train and on towards the Sutpour Mountains. Dhal served with rice, vegetables and a simple salad, eaten using rough rips of chapatti bread to scoop it into your mouth: filling, soothing, wholesome fodder. My great-great-relative Colonel Woodthorpe inspired this recipe, which I found in a family scrapbook. Woodthorpe wandered the undiscovered trails of the Hindu Kush as Queen Victoria's exploring, surveying representative, pasting oddments into his book as he went.

SERVES 4

200g/7oz split red lentils
4 teaspoons vegetable oil
½ a red onion, peeled and chopped
½ teaspoon crushed garlic
1 teaspoon cumin seeds
4 teaspoons dried onion (available from Middle Eastern and Indian stores, though you could increase the amount of fresh onion)
¼ teaspoon ground turmeric
1 teaspoon salt
2.5cm/1 inch piece of fresh ginger, peeled
½ teaspoon cayenne pepper
A handful of fresh coriander, chopped
Juice of ½ a lemon
Chapattis or flatbreads, to serve

Soak the lentils in cold water for a minimum of 1 hour, then drain them well and set aside.

Put the oil into a medium pan and heat gently. Add the chopped onion and garlic and when the onion is browned, add the cumin seeds and dried onion.

Put the lentils into a separate pan and add water to cover them by 2.5cm/1 inch or so. Add the turmeric, salt, ginger and cayenne. Bring to the boil, then reduce the heat and simmer until the lentils are soft and soupy, stirring occasionally. Skim off any foam that has gathered on top of the lentils during cooking.

Next, add your onion mixture to the lentils and gently stir everything together, adding the chopped coriander and lemon juice as you go.

Serve with chapattis or flatbreads.

Rosie Scott
BOTI KEBABS

Boti kebabs are a popular Mughlai dish made with lamb. Traditionally the whole lamb's leg muscle is marinated overnight in spiced yoghurt, then speared with metal skewers and cooked slowly over hot embers. You can also cook the kebabs in the oven or you could try them on a small charcoal burner. You may not find yourself faced with an imminent elephant ride, like Mr Fogg, but these juicy, soft morsels should fortify you against any smaller hurdles that life throws into your path.

SERVES 4

900g/2lb lean sirloin steak
   or lamb leg meat
60ml/2fl oz vegetable oil
6 tablespoons chopped fresh
   coriander, to serve

For the marinade
110g/4oz yoghurt
3 tablespoons chopped onion
1 tablespoon water
2 teaspoons salt
2 teaspoons poppy seeds
2 teaspoons minced garlic
1 teaspoon ground ginger
4 teaspoons ground coriander
2 teaspoons ground turmeric
½ teaspoon ground cumin
¼ teaspoon cayenne pepper

Suggestions for the skewers
2 small green peppers, each cut
   into 8 pieces, or 1 large green
   pepper, cut into 16 pieces
1 large red onion, cut into
   16 pieces
16 mushrooms

To serve
4 tablespoons plain yoghurt
Juice of 1 lemon
1 tablespoon poppy seeds
A handful of fresh mint leaves

Cut the meat into 4cm/1½ inch pieces and place them in a bowl. Pour boiling water over them and leave them to soak for 5 minutes. Drain well and place in a clean bowl.

Add the marinade ingredients to the bowl and mix well with your hands to make sure the meat is seasoned and coated on all sides. Cover with clingfilm and pop into the fridge to marinate for 5 hours, or overnight.

When the meat is ready you can begin to construct your kebabs, alternating pieces of meat with whatever other suggested ingredients you are using until the skewer is splendid.

Cook over a slow-burning charcoal fire until the meat is browned and tender, basting frequently with the marinade and the oil.

If you are cooking the kebabs in the oven, preheat it to 220°C/425°F/gas mark 7. Place the kebabs in a non-stick ovenproof tray, cover them with foil and bake for about 20 minutes. Remove the foil and baste the kebabs with the marinade, then reduce the heat to 180°C/350°F/gas mark 4 and cook for a further 10 minutes, or until the meat is tender.

While the kebabs are cooking, mix together the yoghurt, lemon juice, poppy seeds and mint in a bowl to make a dressing. When the kebabs are ready, remove the skewers and serve the meat in flatbreads, with the yoghurt dressing drizzled over the meat.

FRAGRANT SPICES

'Nutmeg trees in full foliage filled the air with a penetrating perfume'

My violent allergic reaction to the consumption of chillies has meant that I've always erred in favour of the more fragrant spices – the seedy, the barky and the aromatic as opposed to the rooty and the fruity – steering well clear of my *bête noire* and potential assassin, the chilli.

Nutmeg and mace are sister spices. Nutmeg has a sweet flavour, with warm and spicy undertones, whereas mace is more pungent. They both derive from the fruit of *Myristica fragrans*, which has a shiny brown nut at its core. Nestling inside the nut lies a softer kernel (the nutmeg), and covering the nut is a peculiar bright red mesh (the mace). The soft mace is removed, pressed flat, and sun-dried until it turns a pale golden yellow. To obtain the nutmeg, the nuts are sun-dried until brittle and then cracked open with a light hammer blow.

In Fogg's day it was fashionable for a gentleman to carry a wee fold-up nutmeg grater in his top pocket, and a nutmeg around his neck to sniff when it was necessary to cover the hideous stenches that permeated around the sewers and rivers of nineteenth-century London Town. It also allowed for those moments when only a dusting of fresh nutmeg would do, such as over Fogg's hot punch in the Reform Club.

Of the barky variety, cinnamon is probably my most oft-used spice. Mentioned in the Bible, the history of cinnamon is the history of trade itself: it has been fought over and traded for millenia. From it's appearance, it's hard to believe this humble bark has such beautiful depth and flavour.

Coriander, cardamon, caraway and cumin seed provide aromatic hits, while cloves and saffron are my flowery spices of choice. Allspice, a dried berry that closely resembles the mingled fragrances of cinnamon, cloves and nutmeg, and the quite beautiful star anise that comes from the small evergreen magnolia tree, bring up the rear of my spice rack...

Dr Loftus SPICED COOKIES

No tiffin box worthy of the name should be without a cookie or three. So here are three to choose from: one with chewy fruity dates, one with a gingery crunch and one with fragrant cardamom. The perfect snacking food for a long trek and a Loftus family favourite (inherited from my explorer relative Colonel Woodthorpe), these cookies are intensely aromatic: the perfect edible pick-me-up.

BLIND DATE COOKIES

MAKES 36

36 pitted dried dates
36 pecan nuts
½ teaspoon ground nutmeg
1 teaspoon vanilla extract
¼ teaspoon lemon extract
100g/3½oz butter
175g/6oz light brown sugar
1 large free-range egg, beaten
265g/9½oz plain flour
1½ teaspoons baking powder
½ teaspoon sea salt
120ml/4fl oz milk

Preheat the oven to 190C/375°F/gas mark 5 and lightly grease a couple of baking sheets.

Stuff each pitted date with a pecan nut and set aside.

Put the nutmeg, vanilla extract, lemon extract, butter and sugar into a large bowl and mix until well blended. Beat in the egg.

Sift the flour with the baking powder and salt. Now, bit by bit, add alternate spoons of flour and splashes of milk to the bowl, stirring well after each addition until everything has incorporated into a good dolloping dough.

Take a teaspoon and drop rounded half-spoonfuls of dough on to your prepared baking sheets, roughly 5cm/2 inches apart. Press a stuffed date into the centre of each one, then cover the date completely with another half-teaspoonful of dough. Bake in the oven for about 15 minutes, or until the edges are brown.

Whip the cookies out of the oven and put them on a wire rack to cool before eating. Lovely with a cup of coffee.

GUNNING GINGERBREAD COOKIES

MAKES ABOUT 36

1 teaspoon ground nutmeg
½ teaspoon ground cloves
½ teaspoon ground cinnamon
1½ teaspoons ground ginger
1 teaspoon salt
1 teaspoon bicarbonate of soda
100g/3½oz butter
110g/4oz brown sugar
350g/12oz unsulphured
 molasses
1 tablespoon cider vinegar
3 tablespoons water
425g/15oz plain flour, sifted

Preheat your oven to 200°C/400°F/gas mark 6 and lightly grease a baking sheet.

In a large bowl, mix together the nutmeg, cloves, cinnamon, ginger, salt, bicarbonate of soda and butter. Then gradually add the sugar and molasses.

Combine the vinegar and the water in a small bowl, and make sure you have sifted your flour. Then gradually add both to the sugar-and-spice mixture, alternating splashes of liquid with spoonfuls of flour. Mix well until combined into a dough with a soft dropping consistency – not too dry, not too wet.

Using a tablespoon, drop dollops of dough on to your prepared baking sheet, roughly 5cm/2 inches apart. Bake in the oven for 6–8 minutes, or until lightly browned at the edges and just set.

Allow the cookies to sit for a couple of minutes before gently transferring them to a wire rack to cool.

CARDAMOM FORK COOKIES

100g/4oz soft butter or
   margarine
1 teaspoon bicarbonate of soda
½ teaspoon ground cardamom
¼ teaspoon salt
175g/6oz light brown sugar
1 large free-range egg
350g/12oz plain flour, sifted
1 teaspoon cream of tartar

Preheat your oven to 180°C/350°F/gas mark 4 and have ready an ungreased baking sheet.

In a large bowl, combine the butter, bicarbonate of soda, cardamom and salt. Gradually blend in the sugar, then beat in the egg. Use a handheld electric whisk if you have one.

Into a separate bowl, sift together the flour and the cream of tartar. Gradually add these dry ingredients to your other bowl, stirring well until you have a good malleable dough. Place the dough in the fridge and chill for 3–4 hours.

When your dough is ready, use your hands to shape into 1cm/½ inch round balls. Flatten them a bit, then place them on an ungreased baking sheet with about 5cm/2 inches space between each one. Dip a fork into some flour and press down softly into each cookie twice, to form a criss-cross pattern like a mini hedgehog.

Bake in the oven for about 10 minutes, until the cookies are fragrant and golden, then remove and gently transfer them to a wire rack to cool.

Serve old school with a glass of cold milk.

Bella Bellissima
BELLA'S COCKTAILS

Let's not forget to make time for a little libation. There's something particularly wonderful about preparing drinks — the rituals and rhythms we develop for brewing and mixing, straining and pouring into glass or china, with a toast or a clink. The perfumier Bella Bellissima has devoted her life to listening to notes, blending fragrances and creating a bit of magic in a bottle. Her recipes for spiced tea and a champagne cocktail both bring that magic to the glass in a perfect blend of fragrance and flavour.

AROMATIC SPICED TEA

MAKES A LARGE TEAPOTFUL

50g/2oz brown sugar
4 black cardamom pods
1 stick of cinnamon
1 vanilla pod
1 star anise
½ teaspoon mixed spice
1 teaspoon rosewater, to taste
2 tablespoons loose black tea

Lovers, beware: inspired by the rich abundance of the intensely scented spices found on the trail from Persia to India, this aromatic concoction combines ingredients said to have powerful aphrodisiac properties...

Put all the ingredients into your teapot, fill it with hot (but not scalding) water, stir to dissolve the sugar and leave to infuse until the tea is to your liking. Serve in a lovely tea glass, pouring the liquid through a tea strainer. Inhale deeply as you sip.

AOUDA'S CHAMPAGNE COCKTAIL

Aouda is a solitary young Indian woman in danger, saved from certain death on the funeral pyre by the handsome Fogg. She is, as you might expect, a delicate beauty, so perfect in every way that even Fogg's rational head tumbles right over his heels.

FOR 1 COCKTAIL GLASS

A few fresh pomegranate
  kernels
1 teaspoon crème de cassis,
  or crème de framboise
1 teaspoon 100%
  pomegranate juice
½ a glass of champagne
  or prosecco

Let's celebrate giddy heads and fluttering hearts with a combination of champagne bubbles and pomegranate jewels.

Originating in Persia and Mesopotamia, the pomegranate is the symbol of Aphrodite, the possible forbidden fruit of Adam and Eve, and its tree was said to be the tether of the mythical unicorn. Whether you want to win a heart or stoke a flame, this heady, fizzy, seductive concoction is the rather tasty way to go about it.

Pop a few pomegranate rubies into your champagne flute. Then add the cassis or framboise, and the pomegranate juice. Top it all up with bubbles and stir to effervescent life before serving to your amour. The toast is, of course, 'To true love'.

Sarah Tildesley
FRAGRANT BENGALI FISHCAKES

Pushing on towards Bengal, the cuisine of this landscape is known for its subtle yet sometimes fiery flavours and for its use of fish plucked from the fresh-water rivers of the Ganges delta. Sarah Tildesley, probably the best food stylist in the world, makes a chilli-free version for me, but our friends love these hot balls of spicy Bengali deliciousness.

MAKES 16 SMALL CAKES, ENOUGH TO SERVE 4

300g/11oz floury potatoes (such as Maris Piper), peeled and cut into small cubes
300g/11oz boneless, skinless, sustainable white fish fillets
Groundnut oil, enough for shallow frying
2 cloves of garlic, crushed
1–2 fresh green chillies, seeded and very finely chopped
A piece of fresh ginger, approx. 3cm/1¼ inches, finely grated or crushed
1 small onion, very finely chopped
½ teaspoon turmeric
1 teaspoon ground coriander
1 teaspoon ground cinnamon
Sea salt and freshly ground black pepper
A small bunch of fresh coriander, stalks finely chopped
1 egg, beaten
1 tablespoon of plain flour

To serve
Shredded white and red cabbage and sliced red onion, dressed with lime juice and toasted coriander seeds

First, put a steamer over simmering water so it can get nice and hot. When it's ready, put in the potato cubes (keeping a piece back) and cook for 5 minutes, lid in place. Add the fish fillets for a further 3 minutes, or until both are cooked through. Remove and set aside to cool a little. Drain any excess moisture.

Gently heat a glug of the groundnut oil in a frying pan. Add the garlic, chillies, ginger and onion, and sizzle together. Then add all the spices, a generous pinch of salt and pepper, and the finely chopped stalks from your coriander.

Once the onion has softened, add the potato and fish to the frying pan, with another splash of oil if needed, and cook until the ingredients are dry. Mix well to combine, then mash everything together in the pan with a fork. Add the egg, the coriander leaves and the flour and shape into 16 walnut-sized balls.

Heat your groundnut oil for frying – you should aim for the oil to be about 2cm/¾ inch deep in an accommodating frying pan. To test when the oil is ready, take a piece of potato and gently drop it into the hot oil – if it starts to fizz, you're good to go.

Gently squash each ball to form a patty. Don't worry if they break up a little around the edges; it will make the cakes crispy. Fry the patties, very carefully, in batches for 1–2 minutes on each side until golden, then remove with a slotted spoon to transfer them on to kitchen paper.

Anna Jones
PIYAJKOLIR TARKARI: BENGALI PRAWNS

Anna Jones describes the time she ate a version of these Bengali prawns in a beach-side shack in Kerala. The restaurant was just a few pieces of wood thrown together, but these prawns — the size of her hand — were the best spicy, nigella-seedy prawns she's ever had. This recipe for a Bengali version is the closest she has found: having been blown-away by the original, she only remembers the huge amount of spring onions they used — four bunches! This dish is a reminder of how a superior juicy prawn can leave a lobster pink with embarrassment.

SERVES 4

600g/1lb 6oz raw king prawns, peeled and deveined
Sea salt
1 teaspoon ground turmeric
Vegetable or groundnut oil
4 medium potatoes, peeled and cut into cubes
1 tablespoon nigella seeds (kalonji)
3–4 fresh green chillies, cut in half lengthways
4 bunches of spring onions, trimmed and sliced
½ teaspoon chilli powder

Put the prawns into a bowl and season with a pinch of salt. Sprinkle over half the turmeric and stir, then set aside for 15 minutes to marinate.

Put a couple of tablespoons of oil into a large deep frying pan over a high heat. Add the prawns and fry for 2 minutes or so on each side until golden brown, then remove to a plate and set aside.

Add a little more oil to the pan and put back on the heat. Put in the potato cubes and fry until golden, then add the nigella seeds and the chillies. Add the spring onions and cook until lightly browned and softened, then stir in the remaining turmeric, the chilli powder and a little salt.

Pour in a mugful of water, cover with a lid and simmer until the potatoes are cooked through, stirring from time to time and adding more water if it looks too dry.

Return the prawns to the pan and cook for a further minute or so to warm them through. Serve with warm chapattis and simple basmati rice.

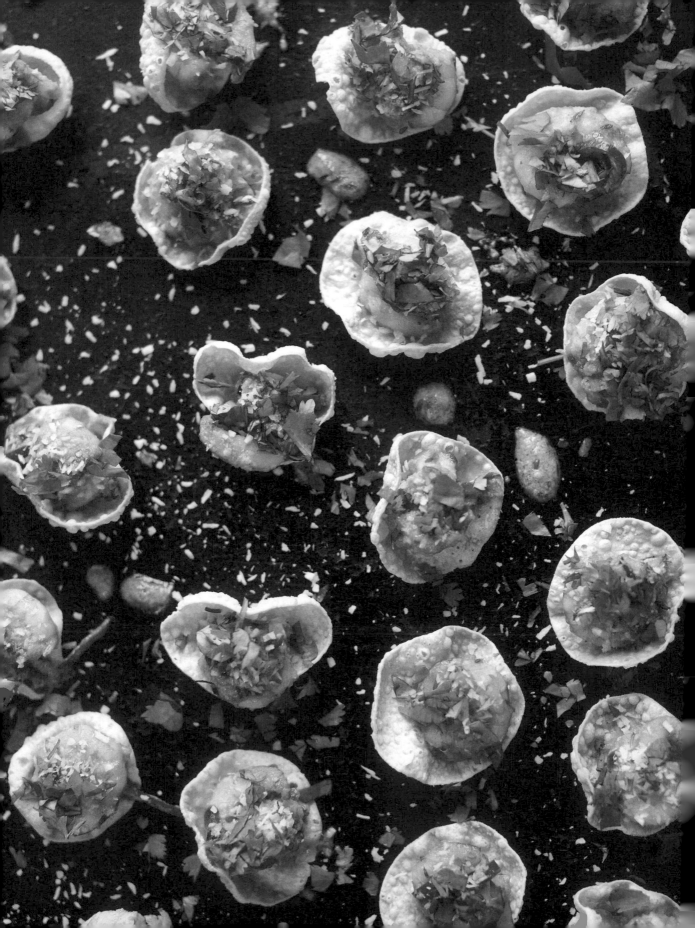

Ravinder Bhogal
MALAI JHINGRI POPPADOMS

When I try to imagine Mrs Aouda, the love of Fogg's life, I think of Ravinder Bhogal. Elegant, beautiful and poised, she's the ideal person to offer a recipe as we begin to plan our departure from Indian shores. There is a popular saying in Bengal: 'Fish makes a Bengali'. For them, the scent of seafood cooking is a memory of home. Poppadoms are normally a quick filler, but here they are transformed into the perfect food for sharing with friends. These 'king crackers', as Ravinder calls them, are topped with gently spiced prawns cooked in coconut milk, the Kolkata way.

MAKES 40

350g/12oz raw tiger prawns
2 teaspoons ground turmeric
Sea salt
A glug of groundnut oil or ghee
1 red onion, chopped
1 teaspoon cumin seeds
3 cardamom pods, bruised
1 stick of cinnamon, broken up
2 whole dried chillies, snapped in half
A pinch of saffron, ground with a tablespoon of warm water
6 cloves, crushed
1 fresh red chilli, chopped
1 tablespoon freshly grated fresh ginger
1 teaspoon sugar
1 tablespoon tomato purée
150ml/5fl oz coconut milk
Juice of ½ a lime
40 mini poppadoms
2 tablespoons chopped fresh coriander
3 tablespoons freshly grated coconut or unsweetened desiccated coconut

Put the prawns into a bowl with a teaspoon of turmeric and some sea salt and leave to marinate for 15 minutes.

Heat the oil or ghee in a frying pan, then add the onion and cook until soft. Sprinkle in the cumin, cardamom, cinnamon, dried chillies, saffron and cloves and continue to fry until the onions are golden brown and the spices fragrant.

Stir in the fresh chilli, ginger, sugar, a pinch of salt, the tomato purée and the remaining turmeric and fry for another minute. Whisk in the coconut milk. Once the mixture has come to a simmer, toss in the prawns. When they are pink and opaque, take off the heat and squeeze in the lime juice. Allow to cool.

To serve, heap the mixture on to mini poppadoms and garnish with the chopped coriander and grated coconut.

Atul Kochhar
NIZAMI SUBJ KATHI: SPICY VEGETABLE WRAPS

Calcutta marks the end of the Indian leg of our travels. From here, the journey will continue on board the *Rangoon*: the P&O liner bound for Hong Kong and the Orient. But before we leave, I think we should mark the occasion with a recipe inspired by the street-food of this teeming city: the wonderful and gentle Atul Kochhar's take on a popular roadside snack created during Muslim rule in East India. Atul serves his wraps with a simple salad of matchsticked cucumber, slices of red onion and tomato, tossed in lemon juice and sprinkled with chilli powder and toasted cumin seeds.

SERVES 4
4 large chapattis or tortillas
3 tablespoons vegetable oil

For the filling
60ml/2½fl oz vegetable oil
1 teaspoon cumin seeds
A small piece of fresh ginger,
   cut into matchsticks
1 teaspoon chopped green chilli
1 red onion, thinly sliced
1 carrot, cut into matchsticks
100g/3½oz white cabbage,
   cut into strips
50g/2oz shiitake mushrooms,
   sliced
1 teaspoon chilli powder
1 teaspoon ground turmeric
1 teaspoon ground coriander
½ teaspoon garam masala
½ teaspoon salt
150g/5oz paneer cheese, cut
   into 0.5cm/¼inch strips
1 tablespoon lemon juice
A handful of chopped coriander

For the batter
50g/2oz gram flour
¼ teaspoon salt
¼ teaspoon chilli powder
¼ teaspoon ground turmeric
A small handful of chopped
   fresh coriander leaves

First make the filling. Heat the oil in a wok, then add the cumin seeds and sauté until they crackle. Add the ginger, green chilli and onion and sauté gently until the onion is softened.

Add the carrot, cabbage and mushrooms, and sauté for a further minute. Add the ground spices and salt, and cook for 2–3 minutes. The vegetables should have softened slightly by now. Add the strips of paneer and lightly toss with the spicy veg.

Remove the wok from the heat and allow the mixture to cool slightly before finally adding the lemon juice and coriander leaves.

Put the gram flour, salt, spices and chopped coriander into a bowl and stir well. Add about 5–6 tablespoons of water and mix to form a smooth thick batter.

To cook the chapattis, heat 3 tablespoons of oil in a large frying pan. One at a time dip the chapattis into the batter and pan-fry for about 1 minute on each side.

Lay out the chapattis on a clean surface and place a good few spoonfuls of spiced vegetables in the centre of each one. Roll up to enclose the filling and serve warm or cold, with the salad alongside.

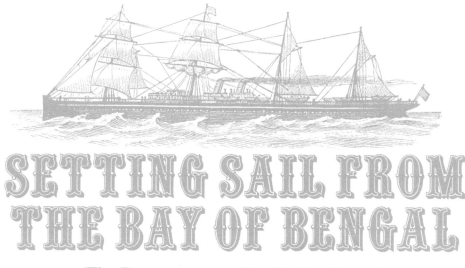

SETTING SAIL FROM THE BAY OF BENGAL

'The *Rangoon* – one of the Peninsular and Oriental Company's boats plying in the Chinese and Japanese seas – was a screw steamer, built of iron, weighing about seventeen hundred and seventy tons, and with engines of four hundred horse-power. She was as fast, but not as well fitted up, as the *Mongolia*, and Aouda was not as comfortably provided for on board of her as Phileas Fogg could have wished. However, the trip from Calcutta to Hong Kong only comprised some three thousand five hundred miles, occupying from ten to twelve days, and the young woman was not difficult to please… Along the coasts swarmed by thousands the precious swallows whose nests furnish a luxurious dish to the tables of the Celestial Empire.'

Sybil Kapoor
SYBIL'S STICKY ORANGE, KASHMIRI CHILLI AND VODKA CAKE

As Fogg, Passepartout and Aouda board the *Rangoon* for the next leg of their journey towards South-East Asia, Sybil Kapoor's amazing cake would provide a welcome taste of luxury. Playing with your palate and toying with your tastebuds, each sticky mouthful of the meltingly light sponge is soused with tangy-sweet syrup and peppered with tiny spikes of chilli and vodka.

SERVES 8-10

170g/6oz softened butter,
    plus extra for greasing
170g/6oz caster sugar
1½ oranges
3 large free-range eggs,
    separated
85g/3oz self-raising
    flour, sifted
85ml/3fl oz dessert wine
85g/3oz ground almonds
1 lemon
30g/1oz granulated sugar
2 dried Kashmiri chillies
3 tablespoons vodka

To decorate and serve
Garnish with the pretty candied zest and the Kashmiri chillies, which you have strained from the syrup, and accompany with some Indian tea

Preheat the oven to 170°C/325°F/gas mark 3 and butter a 20cm/8 inch springform cake tin.

Beat the butter and caster sugar together in a bowl until pale and fluffy. Finely grate the zest of 1 orange, add to the sweetened butter, and then gradually beat in the egg yolks, followed by 2 tablespoons of flour and the dessert wine.

Lightly fold in half the ground almonds, followed by half the remaining flour. Next fold in the remaining ground almonds, then the last of the flour.

Whisk the egg whites in a clean, dry bowl until they form firm peaks. Quickly and gently fold them into the cake mix, then spoon the mixture into your cake tin and place in the centre of the oven.

Bake for 50 minutes, or until a skewer comes out clean. Turn out and place on a cooling rack over a deep-rimmed plate.

Using a potato peeler, finely pare the zest of the lemon and the remaining half orange. Put the zest, granulated sugar, dried chillies and 100ml/3½fl oz of water into a small pan. Place over a low heat to dissolve the sugar, then simmer gently for 10 minutes. Cover, remove from the heat, and leave to infuse. Meanwhile squeeze the juice from 1½ oranges and the lemon and set aside for later.

As soon as the cake is turned out of its tin, return the syrup to the heat and bring to the boil. Add the fruit juices and vodka, and strain the warm liquid into a jug. While the cake is still warm, prick it all over with a fork and then drip the syrup into the cake until it is completely covered. Decorate.

Andy Harris
ANDAMAN ISLAND SQUID AND PINEAPPLE

Having left Calcutta behind, our travellers' four-day journey towards Singapore takes them through the Andaman Islands. Here is a recipe from this archipelago that combines the memory of India and anticipates the approaching Far East. Like its creator, this recipe initially seems quite bonkers, but the impressed and contented murmurs of your friends and family will prove what an exciting dish this is. It's a great alternative to one of my simple favourites: grilled squid with a squeeze of lemon.

SERVES 4

500g/1lb 2oz squid, cleaned
  and sliced
2 cloves of garlic, sliced
50g/2oz fresh ginger, peeled
  and finely chopped
3 tablespoons fish sauce
Sea salt and freshly ground
  black pepper
2 tablespoons peanut or
  vegetable oil
4 spring onions, sliced
½ a fresh pineapple, peeled
  and sliced
2 tablespoons finely chopped
  fresh coriander
1 fresh red chilli, sliced

Put the squid, garlic, ginger and fish sauce into a bowl, and season with a little sea salt and freshly ground black pepper. Leave to marinate for 10–15 minutes.

Heat the oil in a wok over a high heat. When sizzling hot, add the squid and all the marinade ingredients and cook, stirring constantly, for 5–7 minutes, until tender.

Add the spring onions and pineapple, and cook for 3 minutes, until the sauce has thickened.

Finish with half the coriander, chilli and more black pepper. Serve immediately and garnish with the remaining coriander.

ASIA AND THE ORIENT

'The *Rangoon* rapidly approached the Straits of Malacca, which give access to the China seas.'

Jake Tilson
NASI GORENG

The Indonesian island of Sumatra is massively volcanic and its cuisine erupts with big flavours and fragrance. Jake Tilson — artist, writer, designer, broadcaster, photographer and general *bon vivant* — is the man for a Sumatran recipe. The Scottish ancestors of Jake's potter wife, Jeff, were tea planters in Sumatra in the 1920s. Jake has inherited their recipe for Nasi Goreng, which he cooks on a Sunday night using leftover chicken and rice. To make the dish truly Sumatran, you could use seafood rather than chicken: those scary packets of dried little fishes from Asian supermarkets would be perfect.

SERVES 3

2 eggs
1 tablespoon peanut
   or sesame oil
2 onions, finely chopped
2 cloves of garlic, crushed
3cm/1¼ inch fresh ginger,
   finely chopped
1 large fresh chilli, seeded
   and sliced
½ teaspoon ground turmeric
1 teaspoon ground cumin
1 teaspoon ground coriander
2 handfuls of cooked chicken,
   cut into thin strips, or
   cooked beef, sliced (Scottish
   option), or a few handfuls
   of dried/fried small fish
   (Sumatran option)
3 portions of cold cooked rice
1 tablespoon soy sauce
2 tablespoons peanuts

Beat the eggs in a bowl and make a thick omelette in a wide frying pan, cooking the eggs in a little oil until firm. Slice into thin strips and set aside.

Add the peanut oil, onions, garlic, ginger and chilli to the pan and cook gently until the onions are translucent, for about 5 minutes. Then add the turmeric, cumin and coriander, followed by the chicken (or beef, or fish). Stir well and cook over a medium heat for a few minutes.

Break up the cooked rice with a spoon, if it needs it, and add to the pan. Keep stirring until everything is piping hot, for about 5 minutes. Stir in the soy sauce.

Toast the peanuts in a small dry pan on a low heat and garnish your nasi goreng with the nuts and the omelette slices.

No leftover rice? Just add a cup of dry rice to boiling water, cook until tender and cool before using.

Anna Jones
GADO GADO

This is traditional Indonesian street food and normally consists of a vegetable salad with a peanut dressing – which is poured over the salad just before serving. The name literally means 'mix-mix' in Indonesian and the recipe differs from region to region. This is the Anna Jones version, based on her travels and tribulations in South East Asia.

SERVES 2-4

For the sauce
A splash of vegetable oil
2 cloves of garlic, finely
  chopped
3 shallots, finely chopped
1 fresh red chilli, finely chopped
200g/7oz unsalted peanuts
400ml/14fl oz water
50g/2oz palm sugar or
  brown sugar
150ml/5fl oz coconut milk
3 lime leaves
1 teaspoon tamarind paste
2 tablespoons sweet soy sauce

For the vegetable salad
A splash of vegetable oil
200g/7oz tofu, cut into cubes
A handful of green beans,
  trimmed
2 carrots, peeled and thinly
  sliced
A handful of beansprouts,
  washed and drained

For the garnish
4 shallots, finely sliced
1 tablespoon vegetable oil
½ a cucumber, shaved

For the garnish, lightly fry the 4 shallots in the vegetable oil until brown and crisp and set them aside.

To make the sauce, heat the oil in a wok, then add the garlic, shallot, chilli and peanuts and fry for a couple of minutes until they start to brown. Blitz the hot mixture in a food processor, then put it back into the pan, add the rest of the sauce ingredients and simmer for 5 minutes.

To make the vegetable salad, heat a little oil in a pan and fry the tofu until crisp. Plunge the green beans into boiling water for 2–3 minutes, then drain. Put the tofu, beans, carrots and beansprouts into a bowl and toss with the sauce. Serve topped with shaved cucumber and the fried shallots.

Sarah Tildesley
TIDDLY'S CHICKEN LAKSA

Malaysia and its islands are cocooned by seas whose names reveal a great diversity of cultural influences – the Indian Ocean, the Java Sea, the Andaman Sea, the South China Sea. The Malay cuisine speaks directly of these influences, and Singapore (established by the British in the nineteenth century) is probably the hottest part of the Malaysian melting pot.

SERVES 4

2 tablespoons laksa paste
1 400ml tin coconut milk
A bunch of fresh coriander
600ml/1 pint chicken stock
4 skinless, boneless chicken
    thighs
Juice of 2 limes
2 teaspoons grated palm sugar
A splash of fish sauce
200g/7oz purple sprouting
    broccoli, roughly chopped
200g/7oz pak choi, roughly
    chopped
Freshly ground black pepper
200g/7oz straight-to-wok rice
    noodles
2 large handfuls of beansprouts
A small bunch of spring onions,
    sliced as thinly as you can

To serve
A few shallots, Asian if
    possible, finely sliced
A little vegetable oil
Chilli sauce

To start with, lightly fry the sliced shallots in a little vegetable oil until brown and crisp and set them aside.

Put the laksa paste into a pan with a splash of coconut milk and heat gently until the paste starts to release its glorious aroma. Finely slice the stalks of the coriander – reserving the leaves for later – and add to the pan. Cook for a minute or two, then add the remaining coconut milk and the chicken stock and gradually bring to the boil.

While you are waiting, thinly slice the chicken. When the liquid in the pan has reached the boil, add the chicken, turn down the heat and simmer for 10 minutes, until the meat has cooked through.

Add the lime juice, palm sugar, fish sauce, broccoli, pak choi, coriander leaves and a generous grind of pepper. Give it all a stir and leave to simmer for 3–4 minutes, until the greens are cooked to perfection – they should still have a little crunch.

Bring a large pan of water to the boil. Put the noodles into a bowl and pour some of the boiling water over them, enough to cover. Leave for about 3 minutes, then drain. Put the pan back on the heat, bring back to the boil, and add the beansprouts. Drain, then refresh in cold water. Place a pile of noodles in each bowl, and divide the beansprouts and spring onions between the portions. Ladle the liquid and chicken over the top. Finish with a generous sprinkling of the fried shallots and a drizzle of chilli sauce.

Rachel Khoo
WONTONS IN A SMOKY BROTH

My delightful friend Rachel is luckily rather little as she lives in the tiniest of apartments, in which she runs Paris's smallest underground restaurant: *La Petite Cuisine à Paris*. From her family visits to Malaysia she remembers an old Chinese man riding his bike, which he had turned into a mobile kitchen, ringing his bell and shouting, 'Wonton man is here!' People would come out of their houses with empty bowls and return home with bowls of steaming Cantonese dumpling soup… cooler than a Mr Whippy.

SERVES 3–4 AS A STARTER OR 2 AS A LIGHT LUNCH

For the filling
125g/4½oz raw prawns, shelled and deveined
4 tablespoons finely chopped bamboo shoots
1 teaspoon finely chopped spring onion (white part only, save the rest for the soup)
1 teaspoon cornflour
½ teaspoon salt
½ teaspoon sugar
½ teaspoon sesame oil
½ teaspoon dry sherry
A pinch of white pepper

For the wontons
20–25 wonton skins (can be found in Asian supermarkets or bought online)

For the smoky bacon broth
200g/7oz smoky bacon
1 teaspoon salt
A pinch of sugar
1 litre/1¾ pints cold water

To serve
1 spring onion, finely sliced
2–4 teaspoons light soy sauce
Chilli sauce

Mince the prawns and mix with the rest of the filling ingredients. You can make the filling up to a day in advance and keep it in an airtight container in the fridge. Moisten the edges of one of the wonton skins with a little water and place a teaspoon of filling into the centre. Twist to seal the edges – the wonton should resemble a money bag. Repeat until all the filling is used.

Put the smoky bacon, salt, sugar and water into a pan over a medium heat and bring to the boil. Reduce the heat and simmer for 30 minutes, then pour the liquid through a fine sieve to remove the bacon and little bits.

Bring the strained broth to a simmer again and add the wontons. Cook for 5 minutes. Divide the soup and dumplings between your bowls and garnish with finely sliced spring onions and a drizzle of soy sauce. For a spicy kick, serve with chilli sauce.

If you're having this as a light lunch, add some roughly sliced pak choi or other green leafy vegetables of your choice to the broth at the same time as cooking the wontons.

Guy Botham
SINGAPORE SLING

Fogg and his companions are surrounded by the tropical fruits of Singapore, and this delicious fruity concoction originally hails from the Long Bar of Singapore's Raffles Hotel sometime during the infant years of the twentieth century. The recipe was given to me by my pal Guy Botham, who learnt his craft bar-keeping in Hong Kong before becoming a Hollywood movie producer. This is one of those drinks. Life becomes soft-focus, a piano tinkles in the background, there's a full moon rising, romance is in the air, and it's a long way till dawn… Drink slowly.

SERVES 1
30ml/1fl oz gin
15ml/½fl oz cherry brandy
100ml/4fl oz pineapple juice,
    preferably Sarawak variety
15ml/½fl oz fresh lime juice
1½ teaspoons Cointreau
1½ teaspoons Benedictine
2 teaspoons grenadine syrup
A dash of Angostura bitters

To garnish
Pineapple and a
    Maraschino cherry

Combine all the ingredients in a cocktail shaker, fill with ice, and shake. When the shaker is frosted over, strain the contents into a tall glass. Slide a golden diamond of Sarawak pineapple on to the rim, and place a Maraschino cherry on top. Pretty in pink.

Andy Harris' CHILLI CRAB

Whenever I think of crab, I think of Mr Harris. I've sat on many a beautiful beach or boat or slipway, quietly reading, with him unable to sit still and disappearing between the seaside rocks in search of crab and octopus. This Singaporean recipe is one of his best.

SERVES 4–6

2 tablespoons vegetable oil
4 cloves of garlic, peeled
   and chopped
1 long fresh red chilli,
   seeded and thinly sliced
1 knob of fresh ginger,
   peeled and grated
2 medium-sized crabs, cleaned
   and chopped into large pieces
1 tablespoon sambal oelek
   chilli sauce
1 tablespoon granulated sugar
2 tablespoons soy sauce
Freshly ground black pepper
3 spring onions, finely chopped
1 tablespoon cornflour

To serve
Plain boiled rice
Fresh coriander leaves

Heat the oil in a large wok over a medium heat. Add the garlic, chilli and ginger, and sauté until softened and turning a golden colour.

Add the pieces of crab and cook for about 5 minutes, stirring all the time, then add the chilli sauce, sugar, soy sauce and half a glass of water. Season with freshly ground black pepper and continue to cook for 10 minutes, or until the crab shells become bright orange in colour.

Finally, add the spring onions and cornflour and continue to cook, stirring constantly, until the sauce thickens. Serve immediately, with plain boiled rice and a sprinkling of coriander leaves.

Tip: use crab picks and crackers to get to the meat – a messy but very satisfying meal.

Anna Jones
COCONUT, NUTMEG AND PISTACHIO ICE CREAM CRUNCH BOMBS

This recipe has all the flavours of the East — the deep warming spice of nutmeg, the freshening zing of lime and the palm beach creaminess of coconut — topped off with a crunch from the praline.

SERVES 6–8

For the ice cream
3 egg yolks
1 teaspoon cornflour
4 tablespoons golden caster
   sugar
1 x 400ml tin of coconut milk
500ml/17fl oz double cream

For the pistachio praline
Vegetable or groundnut oil
100g/3½oz shelled, unsalted
   pistachios
100g/3½oz golden caster sugar

To serve
1 whole nutmeg
1 lime
A handful of coconut shavings

In a big mixing bowl whisk the egg yolks, cornflour and sugar together until pale and creamy. Heat the coconut milk in a pan, taking it off the heat just before it boils. Whisk the hot coconut milk into the egg yolk mixture, return to the pan on a low heat and whisk for a couple of minutes until it has thickened slightly. Allow the mixture to cool.

Put the cream into a mixing bowl and whip until peaks form. Fold in the coconut milk mixture. If you have an ice cream maker, put the mixture in and churn. If not, transfer it to a chilled metal container and freeze for 2 hours, then whisk to break down the ice crystals. Put the mixture back into the freezer in the chilled container and repeat the process again after 2 hours.

To make the pistachio praline, scatter the pistachios in the centre of a greased baking tray. Put the sugar into a heavy-based pan with 100ml/4fl oz of water and place over a medium heat. Allow the sugar to dissolve and turn golden around the edges, avoiding the temptation to stir it, until the sugar turns an even shade of rusty caramel. Working quickly, but carefully, pour the caramel over the pistachios. When cool, break the praline into pieces and either whiz in a food processor or place inside a clean tea towel and bash with a rolling pin.

Finely grate the nutmeg and lime zest on to a tray. Scatter the praline dust alongside, then pop the ice cream on the tray and take it to the table. Get everyone to drop their scoops of ice cream into the lime and nutmeg mixture, then repeat with the praline. Top each bowl of ice cream with a sprinkling of coconut.

Jody Vassallo
VIETNAMESE SPRING ROLLS

The *Rangoon* sets sail from Singapore on the South China Sea bound for Hong Kong — a journey that takes the travelling companions past Vietnam. The seas are rough and stormy, which slows their progress, but Fogg remains robust and focused. One imagines him eating a modest supper while fellow passengers wobble around him, green about the gills. These are simply rocking good rolls, first made for me to photograph (and then eat!) on the deck of my boat, *Candy Coloured Tangerine*, by the adorable Jody Vassallo — Australian expert on all things noodley and all food Vietnamese.

MAKES 12 ROLLS

100g/3½oz dried rice vermicelli
8 dried Chinese mushrooms
200g/7oz firm tofu, diced
1 tablespoon grated fresh
 ginger
½ teaspoon five-spice powder
1 large carrot, peeled and cut
 into fine matchsticks
A small bunch of fresh mint
 leaves, finely chopped
12 round rice paper wrappers
 (approx. 22cm/8½ inches
 diameter)
1 tablespoon white wine
 vinegar
3 tablespoons hoi sin sauce
1 teaspoon chilli sauce

Pop the rice vermicelli into a bowl and cover with boiling water. Allow to stand for 10 minutes, or until soft. Rinse, drain well, and pat dry with kitchen paper.

Put the mushrooms into a separate bowl and cover them with 100ml/4fl oz of boiling water. Allow to stand for 10 minutes, or until soft. Strain the liquid into a container and put to one side. Remove the stems from the mushrooms, and cut the caps into fine slices. Put the tofu, ginger and five-spice into the mushroom liquid. Leave to marinate for 10 minutes, then drain, discarding the liquid.

Put the rice vermicelli, carrot, mushrooms and mint into a bowl and gently stir to combine.

Now you can prepare your rice papers and assemble the rolls, one at a time. This is how you do it. First, fill a shallow bowl with warm water and add the white wine vinegar. Take a rice paper wrapper and soak it in the vinegar water until soft. Put the wrapper on a flat, dry surface. Place a heaped tablespoon of the vermicelli mixture on the wrapper, along with a few pieces of tofu. And then you're ready to roll! The easiest way is to fold the edges in to envelop your filling slightly, and then gently roll up the parcel.

When all your rolls are ready, make a dressing by whisking together the hoi sin sauce and chilli sauce.

The rolls can be served fresh or you can deep-fry them in hot oil until crisp and golden. Serve with the dressing in a bowl, the better to dunk the ends into.

Adam Perry Lang
APL'S BEEF BACK RIBS

Fogg, Passepartout and Aouda prepare to disembark among 'the flotilla of junks, tankas and fishing boats which crowd the harbour of Hong Kong', enclosed on one side by the Canton River and on the other by the South China Sea. A final hearty meal on deck above these watery surroundings: APL's beef back ribs. Adam Perry Lang is a BBQ chef extraordinaire and a world expert on cooking meat with fire. No one does it better or with more passion.

SERVES 4–6

250ml/8fl oz dark soy sauce
125ml/4fl oz water
050g/12on sugar
55ml/2fl oz hoisin sauce
8 large cloves of garlic, crushed
2kg/4.4lbs beef back ribs

Whisk the soy sauce, water, sugar, hoisin sauce and crushed garlic together and add to a marinating bag.

Place one rack of ribs in the bag. If the ribs are too large, cut them in half through the meat, rather than the bone, to fit. Seal the bag, distribute the liquid and place in the fridge for 24 hours.

When the ribs are ready to cook, take them out of the bag and place them either in the basket of a large steamer, or in two separate smaller ones. Saving the marinade, bring it to the boil and then simmer in a small pan for 5 minutes.

Steam the ribs gently for 1 hour and 15 minutes, or until tender. Preheat the oven to 190°C/375°F/gas mark 5. When the cooking time is up, remove the meat gently from the steamer.

Place the ribs on a rack in the oven, with a pan of water underneath. Brush the ribs with half of the reserved marinade and cook in the oven for half an hour, or until the meat begins to develop a beautiful roasted brown colour.

When the ribs are cooked, remove them from the oven, brush the top sides with the remaining marinade one final time, and pop under a hot grill for a few minutes, top side up, until crisp and sizzling.

Let the ribs rest for 5 minutes, then serve, with fingerbowls and napkins.

David Loftus
POPPY SEED FRENCH TOAST

Passepartout's wander around Hong Kong's Victoria port, with its 'confused mass of ships of all nations' leads him into a nearby tavern, where the effects of *Papaver somniferum* — the 'sleep-bearing poppy' — are very much in evidence. Passepartout, intoxicated by the effects of liquor, accepts one of the pipes on offer: 'he took it, put it between his lips, lit it, drew several puffs, and his head, becoming heavy under the influence of the narcotic, fell upon the table'. The reviving effect of this poppy seed French toast on the poppy-drunk Frenchman would certainly have been welcome...

SERVES 6 (OR 1 HUNGOVER PASSEPARTOUT)

4 large eggs, beaten
250ml/8fl oz milk
A large pinch of salt
2 tablespoons poppy seeds
1 tablespoon honey
12 slices of firm-textured
   bread
Butter

To serve
Crispy bacon on the side
Honey or maple syrup

Put the eggs, milk, salt, poppy seeds and honey into a bowl and beat until well mixed.

Dip the bread into the batter one slice at a time until covered and plump. Have a frying pan at the ready, with a little melted butter on the go. Flop the bread into the pan and fry on both sides until golden brown.

Serve your toast with a pile of crispy bacon and a drizzle of clear honey or maple syrup.

Jamie Oliver
SWEET DUCK LEGS COOKED WITH STAR ANISE

Fogg and Aouda return to their hotel and dine 'at a sumptuously served *table d'hôte*'. What could be more sumptuous than Jamie Oliver's sweet duck legs? The warming taste of the star anise and cinnamon against the rich plummy meat of the duck is just a delight. Jamie cooked this for me on my boat with the sound of the Thames lapping and the London ducks mournfully quacking beside it.

SERVES 4

4 fat duck legs
4 tablespoons soy sauce
3 teaspoons five-spice
A handful of star anise
½ a stick of cinnamon
1 tablespoon olive oil
1–2 fresh red chillies,
    seeded and sliced
16 plums, halved
    and stoned
2 tablespoons
    demerara sugar

First find yourself a large sandwich bag, or a freezer bag. Pop in the duck legs, soy sauce, five-spice, star anise, cinnamon and olive oil and mush it all around in the bag until the meat is well coated. Leave to marinate in the fridge for between 2 hours and 2 days.

When you're ready to cook the meat, preheat your oven to 170°C/325°F/gas mark 3. Place the chillies, plums and sugar in the bottom of a deep pan or roasting tray, then ease the marinade out of the bag and over the top of the fruit. Mix it all together with your fingers, then place the duck legs on top.

Put the pan or tray into the oven for 2–2½ hours, until the meat falls away from the bone and the pan is full of a rich, jammy, chunky plum sauce. Remove the star anise and cinnamon, and taste the sauce to see if it needs a little more soy. Trust your tastebuds.

Serve with some simple rice or noodles to soak up all the yummy plummy juices.

Sarah Tildesley
COCONUT, LIME AND MINT GRANITA

As the travellers set out into the China Seas on the graceful *Tankadere*, they are nearly halfway through their journey and moving swiftly towards Japan. A refreshing granita to lift travel-weary spirits is in order, and Tiddly is the Queen of the Granita-makers.

SERVES 4, IN SMALL MARTINI GLASSES

200ml/7oz golden caster sugar
500ml/17fl oz water
4 limes, washed well
200ml/7fl oz coconut milk
A bunch of fresh mint, leaves picked

Put the sugar and water into a large pan and warm gently until the sugar has dissolved. When you have reached this point, add the zest of 2 of the limes and the juice of all 4.

Turn off the heat and allow the liquid to cool a little, then carefully pour into a liquidizer (or use a stick blender). Add the coconut milk and mint leaves and blitz until smooth.

Pour the liquid into a shallow dish – a metal dish is best if you have one – and put it into the freezer. After 2 hours, take the granita out and rake through the surface of the ice using a fork, working from the outside in, until you have a tray of light, fluffy ice-flakes, a little paler in colour than when frozen solid.

Pop the granita back into the freezer for an hour, then serve in shallow dishes or glasses with pretty leaves of bright green mint on top.

JAPAN

'There Passepartout saw dazzling
camellias expanding themselves, with
flowers which were giving forth their last
colours and perfumes, not on bushes, but
on trees; and within bamboo enclosures,
cherry, plum, and apple trees, which the
Japanese cultivate rather for their
blossoms than their fruit, and which
queerly-fashioned grinning scarecrows
protected from the sparrows, pigeons,
ravens, and other voracious birds.'

Jody Vassallo
JODY'S GREEN TEA
NOODLES WITH TOFU

Time to relax after a rather stormy passage to Japan. Before arrival in Yokohama, Passepartout ate 'as generously as if Japan were a desert, where nothing to eat was to be looked for'. He needn't have worried. The green tea noodles for this recipe might prove elusive but you can find them online or in Japanese grocers. But if you draw a blank, here's a tip: you can use ordinary soba noodles and add a couple of green tea bags to the boiling water when you're cooking them.

SERVES 4

200g/7oz dried green
   tea noodles
1 tablespoon vegetable oil
1 tablespoon freshly
   grated ginger
300g/11oz firm tofu, cut
   into 2cm/¾ inch cubes
100g/3½oz frozen soya beans
3 tablespoons soy sauce
2 tablespoons mirin
   (Japanese rice wine)
2 tablespoons sake
1 tablespoons caster sugar
50g/2oz butter

Bring a large pan of water to the boil and add the noodles, stirring to prevent them sticking together. Once the water has returned to the boil, add a cupful of cold water and cook for 6–8 minutes, or until the noodles are soft. Rinse under cold water and drain well.

Heat the oil in a wok. Add the ginger and tofu and stir-fry over a medium heat for 5 minutes, or until the tofu is nicely golden brown. Add the frozen beans, soy sauce, mirin, sake and caster sugar, and simmer for a further 3 minutes, or until the beans are soft. Whisk in the butter.

Divide the noodles between 4 bowls, arranging them into gorgeous greenish nests. Place a serving of the tofu bean mixture on each nest, and eat with friends and chopsticks.

Sybil Kapoor
SWEET SPICED BEEF WITH GREEN BEANS

Served with a clever green bean salad, this sweet spiced beef was inspired by the idea of fusing Japanese and Chinese flavours with traditional British cuisine. Marinating the beef in a flavoured sugar and salt mixture gives a succulent and firm texture. One should never quibble with Sybil.

SERVES 4

170g/6oz light
    muscovado sugar
155g/5½oz coarse sea salt
1½ teaspoons ground star anise
1½ tablespoons finely chopped
    fresh ginger
3 cloves of garlic, finely
    chopped
Zest of 2 lemons, finely grated
1–2 fresh red chillies,
    finely sliced
115ml/4oz Kikkoman
    soy sauce
115ml/4oz toasted
    sesame oil
450g/1lb trimmed fillet of beef
2 tablespoons sunflower oil

For the salad
350g/12oz fine green
    beans, trimmed
3 heads of red chicory,
    or 2 handfuls of shredded
    red cabbage
1 red onion, finely sliced
    into rings
A generous ½ teaspoon
    runny honey
1 clove of garlic, finely chopped
1 generous tablespoon
    lemon juice
3 tablespoons walnut oil
Sea salt and freshly ground
    black pepper

Mix the sugar, salt, star anise, ginger, garlic, lemon zest, chillies, soy sauce and sesame oil in a dish large enough to hold the beef. Add the beef and turn to coat thoroughly in the sweet marinade. Cover and place in the fridge for at least 36 hours, turning the meat every 12 hours and rubbing the marinade into the flesh before returning it to the fridge.

After 36 hours, remove the beef and quickly rinse under cold water. Pat dry with kitchen paper. Preheat the oven to 200°C/400°F/gas mark 6.

As soon as the oven is hot, heat the sunflower oil in a non-stick frying pan over a medium flame. As soon as it is hot, add the beef. Colour and sear on all sides, then transfer to a small roasting tray or baking dish. Pour over the frying oil, and place the dish in the oven. Roast for 12 minutes. Remove, cool, and chill until required.

Shortly before serving, make the salad. Drop the green beans into a pan of boiling water and cook for 6 minutes, or until tender. Drain and set aside to cool. Now wash the chicory leaves, and tear them into large pieces. Place in a large bowl with the cooked beans and red onion rings.

Make a dressing by whisking together the honey, garlic, lemon juice and walnut oil. Season and toss everything together. Divide the salad between four plates and top with generous slices of the beef.

Pete Begg
CRISPY TEMPURA

This is one of the easiest things you can make. Tempura batter is the opposite of a normal batter in that you mix it at the last minute and you deliberately make it lumpy! Although this sounds a little strange, if you don't make it like that, it won't work properly. Don't be tempted to use a whisk, as that'll do too good a job. In Japan, tempura chefs use chopsticks to mix their batter, to make sure it doesn't end up too smooth.

ENOUGH FOR A SMALL BOWL OF DELICIOUS BITES

1 egg yolk
240ml/8 fl oz iced water
150g/5oz plain flour –
    Italian '00' works well

Put the egg yolk into a mixing bowl and add the iced water. Swirl your chopsticks in the bowl just enough to ripple the yolk into the water, no more.

Sieve in the flour and stir with the chopsticks for about 20 seconds, making sure you have a half-mixed batter with actual lumps of flour in the liquid and around the edge.

Your batter is now ready to use!

All manner of things can be fried in a tempura batter, from slices of mushroom, onion, leek and sweet potato, to courgette flowers, shiso leaves, prawn tails, stalks of baby ginger, small fish fillets and anything else that takes your fancy. Simply dredge in flour first, dip briefly in the tempura batter, shake off the excess and deep-fry in hot oil for a minute or two.

YOKOHAMA
CARPACCIO

Jamie Oliver and Gennaro Contaldo
YOKOHAMA CARPACCIO

As Fogg prepares to set sail for America, here are two fish carpaccio recipes to bid farewell to Japan and the Far East. The first is an amazing recipe for mackerel that includes the magical combination of pomegranate, lime and tequila; the second, a refreshingly light and tangy starter, especially good for a Christmas table. Both are very easy to make if you adhere to two rules of thumb: use the very best, freshest fish you can get hold of and use your sharpest paring knife to slice it.

JAMIE OLIVER'S FRESH MACKEREL COOKED IN POMEGRANATE, LIME JUICE AND TEQUILA

SERVES 4

275ml/½ pint white
   wine vinegar
Sea salt
1 large mackerel, cleaned,
   pin-boned and filleted
   into 2 fillets
3 ripe pomegranates
Zest and juice of 2 limes
2 shots of tequila
1 teaspoon sesame oil
1 teaspoon grated fresh ginger
2 bulbs of fennel, finely sliced
Extra virgin olive oil

Put the vinegar into a pan with a heaped teaspoon of sea salt and heat until lukewarm, then remove from the heat. Put the mackerel fillets into a tight-fitting dish and cover with the vinegar. Set aside for the next 7 hours… Yes, so start early! When the time is up, drain off the vinegar and set the fish aside while you make a second bath for them as follows.

Juice 2 of the pomegranates by squeezing them into a sieve placed over a bowl. Prepare to work every last drop from the pips (and get covered in sticky ruby juices). When that's ready, add the lime juice, tequila, sesame oil and ginger.

Place the mackerel fillets in a dish with half the juice mixture, turning them to make sure both sides of the fish are covered, and allow them to sit for 30 minutes. This will 'cold cook' the fish.

Drain the mackerel and pat it dry. Slice the fish as thin as you like, and arrange on a serving plate. Make a salad with the finely sliced fennel and the seeds from the third pomegranate, and place on top of the mackerel. Pour over the other half of the juice mixture, and serve with a drizzle of good extra virgin olive oil.

GENNARO CONTALDO'S CARPACCIO DI BRANZINO CON POMPELMO ROSA

SERVES 4

400g/14oz freshest sea
  bass fillet
Juice of 1 pink grapefruit
4 tablespoons extra virgin
  olive oil
Sea salt and freshly
  ground black pepper
2 pink grapefruit, cut into
  segments, pith removed
A handful of salad leaves,
  to serve

Using a sharp paring knife, cut very thin slivers of sea bass, from head to tail. Place them between sheets of greaseproof paper and gently flatten them. Place the slices on a plate, and set aside.

Put the fresh grapefruit juice, 1 tablespoon of olive oil and some salt and pepper into a small mixing bowl and whisk together. Gradually add the rest of the olive oil, and continue to whisk until the sauce begins to thicken. Pour the sauce over the fish and leave for about an hour, in a cool place.

When you are ready to serve, arrange the fish slices on individual plates, with the grapefruit segments and some salad leaves. Drizzle with a simple olive oil dressing, if you fancy.

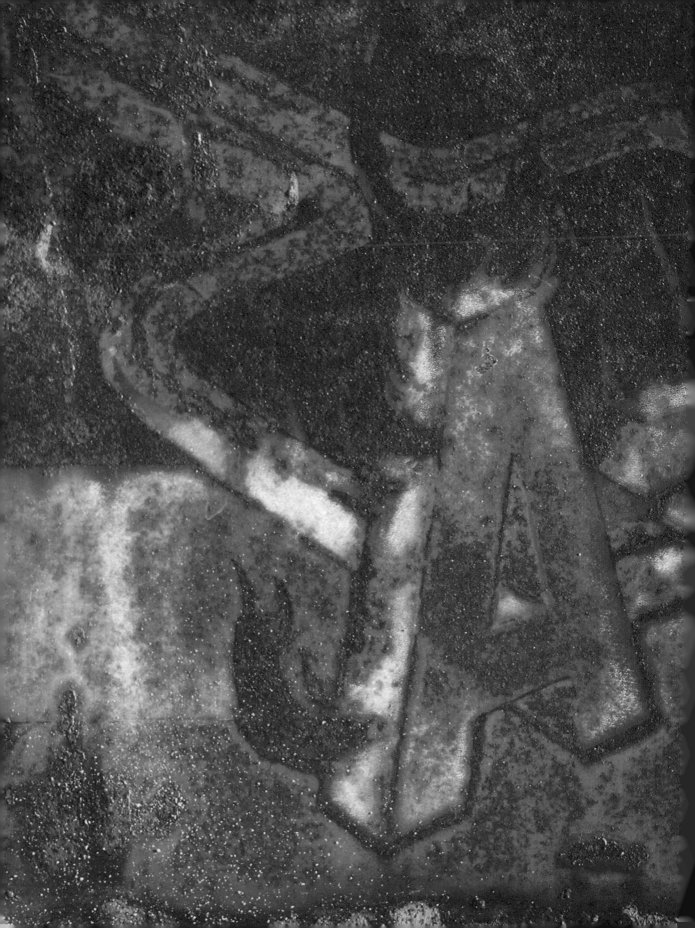

AMERICA

'Nothing of moment happened on the voyage; the steamer, sustained on its large paddles, rolled but little. The "Pacific" almost justified its name… On the ninth day after leaving Yokohama, Phileas Fogg had traversed exactly one half of the terrestrial globe. The *General Grant* passed, on the 23rd of November, the one hundred and eightieth meridian, and was at the very antipodes of London.'

SAN FRANCISCO

'On the 3rd of December, the *General Grant*
entered the bay of the Golden Gate, and
reached San Francisco. . . Passepartout,
in his joy on reaching at last the American
continent, thought he would manifest it by
executing a perilous vault in fine style.'

David Loftus
CHILLED MINTED CUCUMBER AND HONEYDEW SOUP

During the halcyon years of the late nineteenth and early twentieth century, San Francisco had 'a bit of a reputation'. It was widely known as an intoxicating place to be: a city full of saloons, speakeasies, and good-time boys and gals. Folks in the fast set lived topsy-turvy lives — all cocktail breakfasts at lunchtime, and hoochy suppers at three in the morning. How things change. Nowadays, San Fran is a kind of Mecca for healthy living and good karma. I'm not sure Fogg would have approved of either.

SERVES 4

1 large cucumber,
   cut into pieces
1 ripe and sweet honeydew
   melon, cut into pieces
250g/9oz plain low-fat yoghurt
A handful of fresh mint leaves
2 tablespoons fresh lime juice
Zest of ½ a small lime
Salt and freshly ground
   black pepper
A large handful of ice cubes

Pop all the ingredients into a liquidizer with a big handful of ice and blend until smooth to make a refreshing chilled soup for a hot summer's lunch. Check the seasoning, add salt and pepper if necessary, and serve with a few ice cubes.

Alice Waters
LOVAGE BURGERS

Lovage, sometimes known as 'love parsley', is a toothsome and distinctive herb. It tastes a little like celery, with undertones of parsley and chervil, and has a latent sweetness that you wouldn't necessarily expect. If you've never made its acquaintance, now's your chance, with Alice Waters' San Francisco twist on the classic all-American hamburger.

SERVES 4

4 cloves of garlic,
   roughly chopped
Sea salt and freshly
   ground black pepper
8 lovage leaves,
   coarsely chopped
800g/1¾ lb organic
   minced chuck beef
Focaccia bread
Grilled onions
Dijon mustard
Rocket leaves

In a mortar, pound the garlic with a little salt. Add the lovage leaves and briefly continue to pound. Put the minced beef into a bowl and mix in the garlic and lovage, using your hands. Season generously with salt and pepper.

Divide the burger mixture into four portions, and mould each one into a patty between your palms. It is important to pack the meat well and make sure the edges of the patties are smooth to ensure even cooking. Leave a little concave dimple in the centre of each patty.

Warm up the grill – you're aiming for a medium heat. For a medium-rare burger, grill each patty for about 5 minutes on each side.

Slice your bread. The slices should just match the size of your burger, so trim them a little if necessary. Toast each slice until lightly browned, one side just slightly more crisp than the other.

Now build your burger: take a slice of bread (crisper side down), place the patty on top (dimpled side up), and garnish to your heart's content with grilled onions, a smear of Dijon mustard and some rocket leaves. And that's all, folks.

Jamie Oliver's tip: grow your own lovage – it's super easy. And if you can't find lovage, use the small green leaves that tickle the tops of a celery bunch in its place.

Caesar Cardini
CAESAR SALAD

Caesar Cardini ran a popular joint called Caesar's Place in Tijuana, just over the U.S.-Mexico borderline. Caesar's was popular with Hollywood stars and San Diego socialites, and legend has it that Caesar invented his famous salad during one particularly rowdy weekend of revelry, when the restaurant was full and the kitchen was running short on supplies. The salad may have been an improvisation, invented in Tijuana by an Italian-Mexican, but in 1954 the Society of Epicures in Paris called it 'the greatest recipe to originate from America in fifty years'.

SERVES 1

½ a medium loaf of sourdough bread, ripped into bite-size pieces or cut into cubes
225ml/8fl oz extra virgin olive oil, plus a little for drizzling
Sea salt
4 cloves of garlic, peeled
Juice of 1 good large lemon
6 marinated anchovy fillets (from a jar), plus a few extra to garnish
1 tablespoon French mustard
2 teaspoons Worcestershire sauce
3 heads of romaine lettuce, tougher outer leaves removed
110g/4oz Parmesan cheese, grated
4 eggs, boiled for exactly 4 minutes

Preheat the oven to 180°C/350°F/gas mark 4.

Pop the bread pieces on a baking tray, drizzle with a little extra virgin olive oil, sprinkle with sea salt and place in the oven until crisp and golden brown.

In a blender, whiz together the garlic, lemon juice, anchovies, mustard and Worcestershire sauce. Then, keeping the blender running, gradually add the extra virgin olive oil and whiz until silky.

Tear the lettuce leaves into a bowl and pour over the blended dressing. Sprinkle the cheese and the sourdough croutons over the salad leaves, season with salt and pepper to taste, and toss gently with your (clean!) hands. Finally, just before serving, break the soft-boiled eggs into the bowl and gently toss one last time.

Some like their Caesar salad with a few extra anchovy fillets on top – but the anchovy in the wildly strong dressing may be enough for some, so check with your guests if you aren't sure what side of the anchovy divide they're on.

Domenica Catelli
LEMONY QUINOA WITH SHIITAKE, CHICKEN AND CORIANDER

The oh so beautiful and talented Domenica Catelli – founder, chef and patron of Catelli's in Geyserville, a little wine country town just north of San Francisco – introduced me to this recipe. It's delicious and soothing in a soft, nutty, couscous-esque way and couldn't be easier to prepare.

SERVES 6 SKINNY CALIFORNIANS

350g/12oz quinoa
2 tablespoons extra virgin olive oil
1 medium onion, chopped
3 cloves of garlic, minced
110g/4oz shiitake mushrooms, thinly sliced
2 organic chicken breasts, cut into 5mm/¼ inch pieces
Salt and freshly ground black pepper
1 litre /1¾ pints vegetable or chicken stock
2 medium courgettes, cut into 5mm/¼ inch pieces
Juice of 2 lemons
3 tablespoons toasted sesame seeds
Small bunch fresh coriander leaves, ripped into shreds
Extra virgin olive oil, to drizzle

Toast the quinoa in a dry pan, then rinse it under running water and drain. Heat the oil in a medium pan, then add the onions and garlic and sauté for 1 minute. Add the shiitake mushrooms and cook for a few minutes more.

Add the quinoa and the chicken, season with a pinch of salt and some freshly ground black pepper, and add the stock. Bring to the boil, cover the pan, then reduce the heat to low and cook for 15 minutes, until the ingredients are well combined and the chicken is cooked through.

Remove the lid, and add the courgettes, lemon juice, sesame seeds and three-quarters of the coriander. Turn off the heat underneath the pan, replace the lid on top and leave for 2 minutes more.

Finish with the remaining coriander and a drizzle of good olive oil, and season with salt and pepper.

Tip: toasting the quinoa in a dry pan brings more depth to the flavour.

Daniel O'Connell
SAN FRANCISCO SIDES

Street brawler, poet, journalist, athlete, *littérateur*, humorist, dramatist, novelist, adventurer and chef, Daniel O'Connell founded the great San Francisco Bohemian Club the year that Fogg arrives in town. I suspect that these two men, who lived lives rich in food, drink and travel, would have got on rather well. In 1891, O'Donnell published *The Inner Man: Good Things to Eat and Drink and Where to Get Them*, his guide to the very best edibles of his city. Known for his delicate cookery, O'Donnell made dishes that were described as odes, madrigals and hymns.

ASPARAGUS VINAIGRETTE

SERVES 6 BOHEMIAN CLUB BRAWLERS

½ teaspoon sea salt
½ teaspoon sugar
2 teaspoons Dijon mustard
½ teaspoon paprika
125ml/4fl oz tarragon
  wine vinegar
250ml/8fl oz extra
  virgin olive oil
6 sprinkles of Tabasco
1 clove of garlic, crushed
450g/1lb fresh asparagus
1 tomato, seeded and
  finely chopped
150g/5oz pitted black olives
2 fresh mushrooms,
  finely chopped
1 free-range egg,
  hard-boiled and
  chopped, to garnish

Put the salt, sugar, mustard and paprika into a bowl and stir to combine. Add the vinegar, olive oil, Tabasco and garlic, mixing well.

Lightly griddle the asparagus on a hot dry griddle pan for a few minutes, turning it a couple of times. Let it cool, then place it in a shallow dish with the tomatoes, olives and mushrooms and pour over the vinaigrette dressing. Cover, and set aside in the fridge to marinate for about an hour.

When you are ready to serve, remove the vegetables from the fridge, drain, and serve chilled, garnished with the hard-boiled egg.

SAN FRANCISCO SPICY BEETS

SERVES THE SAME 6 BOHEMIAN CLUB BRAWLERS

150ml/5fl oz white
    wine vinegar
2 allspice berries
1 cinnamon stick
6 cloves
2 red beetroots
2 golden/yellow beetroots
2 candy cane beetroots
A handful of fresh
    tarragon leaves
Salt and freshly ground
    black pepper
Extra virgin olive oil

Put the vinegar into a pan with the spices, tarragon and sugar, bring to the boil, then simmer for a couple of minutes and remove from the heat. Peel and then finely slice all the beets, using a speed peeler or a mandolin, and place in a bowl. Cover with the strained spiced vinegar.

Sprinkle the beets with a few tarragon leaves, salt and pepper and drizzle with olive oil.

Tip: to give a deeper flavour to a hollandaise sauce or salad dressing, put 3 or 4 sprigs of the fresh tarragon, along with the spices, into a bottle of white wine vinegar and leave for at least a couple of weeks before using.

TO NEW YORK ON THE PACIFIC EXPRESS

"'From ocean to ocean" – so say the Americans;
and these four words compose the general
designation of the "great trunk line" which
crosses the entire width of the United
States… New York and San Francisco are
thus united by an uninterrupted metal ribbon,
which measures no less than three thousand
seven hundred and eighty-six miles.'

David Loftus
MARINATED FETA WITH WATERMELON, FENNEL AND MINT

Back on the railways again for another epic journey across a continent from coast to coast, taking in Oregon, Utah, Wyoming, Nebraska and finally reaching New York. The food you'll encounter if you travel through America — from east to west, north to south — is far more complex and varied than we generally recognize. Let's leave San Francisco with a taste of East Coast sunshine.

SERVES 6–8

800g/1lb 12oz feta cheese
2 tablespoons unsalted,
  pistachio nuts
A little sunflower oil
1 tablespoon nigella seeds
1 small (1kg/2lb 2oz)
  watermelon, skinned,
  seeded and cubed
2 fennel bulbs, thinly shaved
2 handfuls of fresh flat-leaf
  parsley leaves
1 tablespoon fresh mint leaves

For the marinade
1 tablespoon fresh coriander,
  finely chopped
1 tablespoon fresh mint,
  finely chopped
1 tablespoon thyme or
  oregano, finely chopped
1 small fresh red chilli,
  seeded and finely chopped
Juice and zest of 2 lemons
6 tablespoons extra
  virgin olive oil
2 tablespoons white
  wine vinegar
Freshly ground black pepper

For the dressing
4 tablespoons extra
  virgin olive oil
1½ tablespoons white
  wine vinegar
Sea salt and black pepper

Put the feta into a small shallow bowl. Mix together all the marinade ingredients in a separate bowl and pour over the feta, making sure it is all covered. Season with a little sea salt and black pepper, then cover the bowl with clingfilm and pop it into the fridge for a couple of hours.

Toast the pistachios over a medium heat in a frying pan lightly brushed with sunflower oil. When ready, place them on a clean surface and gently crush them with a rolling pin. Now toast the nigella seeds and add them to the crushed pistachios. Mix together and set aside.

In a salad bowl, toss together the watermelon, fennel shavings, parsley leaves and mint. Make your dressing by putting the olive oil and vinegar into a jar and adding salt and pepper to taste. Shake to combine and pour over the watermelon salad, gently using your fingers to make sure everything is well coated.

When the marinating time is up, remove the feta from its dish, crumble into rough chunks and scatter across your salad. Follow this with a sprinkling of the toasted nuts and seeds for a pleasing final crunch.

Molly Wrigglesworth
MOLLY'S APPLE PIE

A pie to be damn proud of, Auntie Molly's apple pie is a comforting taste of home when you're out of range. I wrote this recipe down directly from Molly's scrapbook. She's over ninety years old: apple pie is clearly essential to a long and happy life.

SERVES 8–10

For the pastry
300g/10oz plain flour
2 tablespoons granulated sugar
1 teaspoon sea salt
175g/6oz unsalted butter,
    cut into 1cm/½inch cubes
    and softened
3–4 tablespoons iced water

For the filling
150g/5oz light brown sugar
3 tablespoons plain flour
½ teaspoon ground cinnamon
½ teaspoon ground cardamom
½ teaspoon ground nutmeg
A pinch of ground ginger
A pinch of sea salt
1kg/2lb 2oz Granny Smith
    apples, peeled, cored
    and sliced
1 tablespoon fresh lemon juice

For the top
1½ tablespoons unsalted
    butter, melted, or
    1 egg, beaten
2 tablespoons caster sugar

Preheat the oven to 200°C/400°F/gas mark 6.

To make the pastry, sift the flour, sugar and salt into a medium-sized bowl. Add the softened butter and mix together (in a blender, with a fork, or by hand) until fully, but coarsely, combined. Slowly add the iced water, bit by bit, stirring until the dough begins to firm up. Go on instinct here – add a little more water if the dough seems too dry. Cover with clingfilm and leave in the fridge for later.

Now make the apple filling. Put the brown sugar, flour, cinnamon, cardamom, nutmeg, ginger and salt into a bowl and mix together. In a separate bowl toss your slices of apple with the lemon juice, then gradually add the sugar and flour mixture and mix well with a metal spoon until the apple is nicely coated with sugar and spices.

Lightly flour a clean, smooth work surface. Take the dough and roll it out into a 40cm/16 inch circle, big enough to blanket a 23cm/9 inch pie dish. Dust the surface with flour, then gently place the dough over the dish and use your fingers to press it carefully into the edges. Allow the excess to hang over the sides.

Fill the pie dish with your spiced apple pieces, and fold the excess dough up and over the filling. Don't worry if it looks higgledy-piggledy. Brush the top with melted butter or beaten egg and sprinkle with caster sugar.

Bake for about 45 minutes, or until the crust is golden brown and the apples are a tender, treacle-and-spice delight. Serve with a scoop of cold vanilla ice cream.

Sybil Kapoor
PAPAYA AND LIME
SALSA WITH LOBSTER

Sybil Kapoor is an amazing writer and broadcaster who always leaves me in a state of awe and admiration. Where Jake Tilson is a 'Man for All Seasons', Sybil is a 'Lady for All Seasons'. She's been a chef in New York and London, and few write about flavour so knowledgeably and eloquently. Papaya and fresh lime combined is possibly my favourite flavour combination of all time, and would certainly form some aspect of my 'last supper'. Sybil has taken those flavours, added habanero chillies, and created a meal for kings.

SERVES 4

1 papaya
1 lime, juiced, plus 2
    extra limes
3 tablespoons finely
    chopped fresh coriander
A pinch of finely diced,
    seeded habanero chilli
Sea salt and freshly
    ground black pepper
4 small boiled lobsters
4 handfuls of mixed
    salad leaves
2 tablespoons good extra
    virgin olive oil

Peel your papaya with a sharp knife. Cut the fruit in half lengthways and scrape out the seeds. Cut the flesh into fine slices and put them into a bowl with the lime juice and coriander. Resist eating there and then! Add the chilli and season with salt and pepper.

Cut each boiled lobster torso in half, lengthways.

Quickly toss the salad leaves in the olive oil. Divide the leaves between four plates, lay the lobster halves on top, and finish with a spoonful of salsa and half a lime per plate. Serve immediately.

Tony Milford, Jr
WILD RICE AND MUSHROOM SOUP

Zizania aquatica, wild rice, is the only cereal that is native to North America and is one of the great glories of the Native Indian northern heartlands. The Ojibway tribe call wild rice 'manomin' and perform dances at pow-wow to celebrate its harvest. It's very wholesome, and very filling. Good fodder for Fogg, then, who is halfway across America, with London in his sights.

SERVES 4–6

800g/11oz wild rice
Salt and freshly ground
    black pepper
50g/2oz unsalted butter
1 large onion, chopped
2 sticks of celery,
    chopped (keep the
    leaves for a garnish)
3 carrots, chopped
110g/4oz mixed mushrooms,
    chopped
3 tablespoons flour
1.2 litres/40fl oz chicken stock
A few sprigs of fresh thyme
3 tablespoons dry sherry
225ml/8fl oz crème fraîche
Extra virgin olive oil to taste

To cook your rice, rinse it well in cold water, and put it into a pan. Cover with water – for every cup of rice you will need 4 cups of water. Add a teaspoon of salt. Bring to the boil, then reduce the heat to low, cover the pan and simmer for 40–50 minutes, until the grains are tender and start to split open. Once ready, drain away any excess liquid and fluff the rice with a fork.

While the rice is cooking, melt the butter in a large pan over a medium high heat. Add the chopped onion, celery and carrots and cook for about 4–5 minutes, stirring, until the vegetables begin to soften. Add the mushrooms and cook for a couple of minutes, until they begin to release some of their liquid. Sprinkle in the flour, stir well and cook for a minute. Add the chicken stock and the thyme, then cover the pan and bring to the boil. Reduce the heat and simmer gently until the vegetables are tender – roughly 15 minutes. Add the sherry and cook for 1 minute more. Remove from the heat and season with salt and pepper. Add the cooked rice to the mixture and stir.

Serve with a dollop of crème fraîche, a sprinkling of celery leaves and a drizzle of extra virgin olive oil.

Alice Waters
POMEGRANATE AND PERSIMMON SALAD

The native American persimmon is a strikingly handsome fruit. Its glossy skin glows vibrant orange like a Jack o'lantern, with a deep-green calyx crown. Inside, the flesh is sweet and almost custardy when ripened — lovely to scoop with a spoon. It's my children's favourite fruit, and I'd say it's a good bet for a fussy little eater. But let's tuck into a jewel-like persimmon and pomegranate salad that's all grown-up. Quite possibly one of the best salads I've ever eaten.

SERVES 4
4 ripe persimmons
4 handfuls of rocket leaves
2 or 3 ripe pomegranates
1 tablespoon sherry vinegar
　or red wine vinegar
3 tablespoons extra
　virgin olive oil
Sea salt and freshly
　ground black pepper
A handful of walnuts

Peel the persimmons, removing the calyces. Some people enjoy the crunchiness of the peel, and so if you're one of those, forget about peeling them and just wash them thoroughly. Either way, slice the persimmons as finely as you can and scatter them on to four small serving plates, accompanying each one with a handful of rocket leaves.

Halve the pomegranates, then hold each half upside down over a bowl and pound the back of the fruit with a wooden spoon, to dislodge as many of the seeds and as much of the juice as possible.

Pick out and discard any of the white pith that may have fallen into the bowl, then sprinkle the seeds over your salad plates, leaving the juice in the bowl. To make a simple vinaigrette, put the vinegar and olive oil into a jar with a pinch of salt and pepper. Add a couple of teaspoons of the pomegranate juice, shake and pour.

Lightly toast the walnuts in a small pan and sprinkle over your lovely salad... yum.

Tony Milford, Jr
BASQUE CHICKEN

Native Indian warriors attack the travellers' train on the Oregon Trail, 'skipping like enraged monkeys over the roofs, thrusting open the doors, and fighting hand to hand with the passengers'. When the armed attackers ride away in defeat, the courageous Passepartout is missing, and Fogg sets off across the plain to rescue him. This recipe for Basque chicken – given to me by Tony Milford of the Navajo Nation – will keep you warm on cold nights, and comfort you in the wilderness.

SERVES 4 NAVAJO INDIANS OR BASQUE SETTLERS

1 tablespoon olive oil
1 free-range chicken,
  cut into 8 pieces
Salt and freshly ground
  black pepper
2 onions, chopped
1 green pepper, seeded
  and sliced
1 red pepper, seeded
  and sliced
3 cloves of garlic, crushed
225ml/8fl oz chicken stock
1 tin of tomatoes
225ml/8fl oz white wine
50ml/2fl oz cognac

Heat the oil in a heavy pan over a medium heat. Sprinkle the chicken pieces with salt and pepper, then put them into the hot pan and cook for about 8 minutes, turning them until they are nicely browned on all sides. Remove the pan from the heat and transfer the chicken to a bowl, leaving the oil in the pan.

Return the pan to the heat, add the onions and peppers, and cook until soft. Stir in the garlic, add the chicken stock, and use a spoon to scrape any brown bits off the bottom of the pan – these will add to the flavour. Add the tomatoes, wine and cognac, stir, then add the chicken pieces.

Loosely cover the pan and simmer over a low to medium heat for about 40 minutes, until the chicken is cooked through and tender. Serve with wild rice.

Deborah Madison
CHERRY AND ALMOND CAKE

The lovely Deborah Madison, ex Chez Panisse chef and lover of great produce, once took me to buy cherries in Santa Fe's glorious farmers' market. My eyes, watering from the chilli fumes in the air, watched as seemingly endless Amtrak trains trundled past the marketplace on a journey with hundreds of miles between stations. Cherries purchased (I remember she had a particular favourite, the orange Royal Annes), she took me home for verbena lemonade and cherry cake. As American as the Fourth of July.

SERVES 8–10

110g/4oz unsalted butter, softened, plus a little for the tin
150g/5oz plain flour, sifted, plus a little for the tin
150g/5oz whole blanched almonds
1 teaspoon baking powder
½ teaspoon sea salt
150g/5oz granulated sugar, plus 1 teaspoon for sprinkling
3 eggs, at room temperature
¼ teaspoon almond extract
½ teaspoon vanilla extract
450g/1lb fresh cherries, pitted
Icing sugar, for dusting

Preheat the oven to 180C/350°F/gas mark 4. Butter a 23cm/9 inch springform cake tin and line the bottom with baking parchment. Flour the sides.

In a food processor (or by hand), coarsely chop the almonds – then take out about a quarter of them and set aside. Add the flour, baking powder and salt to the processor and process until the remaining almonds are finely ground. Transfer to a bowl.

In a food processor (or by hand), cream the butter with the granulated sugar. Add the eggs one at a time, blending each one in fully before adding the next. Add the almond and vanilla extracts.

Add half the flour mixture to the food processor and pulse to blend. Then add the remaining flour mixture and pulse until smooth. Scrape into the prepared tin and place the cherries on top, in a single layer.

Mix the reserved almonds with 1 teaspoon of granulated sugar and sprinkle around the edge of the cake. Bake for around 45 minutes, or until a skewer inserted in the centre comes out clean.

Let the cake cool for 10 minutes, then remove from the tin and allow to cool completely on a wire rack. Dust the top with icing sugar.

MEATLOAF WITH RELISH
David Loftus

Poor Passepartout. Not only does he get himself kidnapped, but because of him the party miss their connecting train to take them on towards Chicago. They find alternative transport though: 'a sledge with sails'. Certainly they'll need a sticks-to-the-ribs sort of snack for the trek and this recipe for a solid stocking-filler is based on time spent with Ardéchoise hunter gatherer Stéphane Reynaud. He's a wonderful big bear of a man, like a boar-munching character from *Asterix the Gaul*.

ENOUGH FOR 1 LOAF, TO SERVE 6

2 large eggs
100ml/4fl oz milk
3 slices of white bread, crusts removed
1 medium onion, finely chopped
150g/5oz chopped celery, with leaves
Olive oil
1 teaspoon fresh thyme leaves
1 teaspoon fresh rosemary leaves
1 teaspoon fresh sage leaves
1 tablespoon Dijon mustard
1½ teaspoons sea salt
½ teaspoon freshly ground black pepper
½ teaspoon ground nutmeg
10 thick slices of smoked bacon, lightly cooked and finely chopped
800g/1lb 12oz minced beef

For the tomato chutney
1 small onion, diced
2 fresh red chillis, deseeded and chopped
1 clove garlic, finely chopped
3 tablespoons extra virgin olive oil
110g/4oz tomato purée
300g/11oz cherry tomatoes
1 teaspoon sugar
150ml red wine vinegar

It's best to prepare the meatloaf mixture the day before cooking, or at least a few of hours before. To make the mixture, beat the egg in a large bowl. Reserve a few dessertspoons of beaten egg and put into the fridge for later. Beat the milk into the remaining egg until well blended. Tear the bread into small pieces and put them into the egg mixture. Set aside to soak for 15 minutes.

Fry the onion and celery in a little oil until soft, adding the fresh rosemary, thyme and sage and frying for five minutes. Put the mustard, salt, pepper, nutmeg, onion, celery and bacon into a bowl and mash the together, using a fork. Add the minced beef and mix thoroughly. Cover the bowl tightly with clingfilm and refrigerate overnight if possible, or for a couple of hours.

When you are ready to cook the meatloaf, preheat the oven to 180°C/350°F/gas mark 4. Take the chilled meatloaf mixture out of the fridge. Turn it out into a loaf tin and place in the oven for 40–50 minutes.

To make the chutney, fry the onion, chilli and garlic in the oil until soft. Add the rest of the chutney ingredients to the pan and cook for 15–20 minutes, until softened and sticky.

Leave the loaf to stand for 5 minutes before serving with the chutney. If you don't do this, you'll find that any attempts at slicing will result in a plate of meat-crumble, rather than meatloaf.

Georgie Socratous
GEORGIE'S BIG GREEK TAVA

The population of Chicago is one of the most diverse in America, and has been ever since the 1840s — and of course this makes for magnificent variety in the food. Wander into Greektown for clever cooking that might look a little like this next dish. A winner from gorgeous Georgie and her Cypriot aunt, it's a wonderful Greek lunch for a family gathering.

SERVES 6

150ml/5fl oz good olive oil

2 large red onions, cut into wedges

2 cloves of garlic, peeled and chopped

1 tablespoon cumin seeds

1kg/2lb 2oz lamb neck fillet, cut into chunks

1kg/2lb 2oz Cyprus or other waxy potatoes, peeled and halved or cut into chunks

1 bay leaf

A small bunch of fresh flat-leaf parsley, chopped

Sea salt and freshly ground black pepper

6 tomatoes, halved

100g/3½oz plain rice

250ml/8fl oz hot stock or water

Preheat your oven to 170°C/325°F/gas mark 3.

Heat a little of the olive oil in a frying pan, then add the onions, garlic and cumin seeds and cook for around 10 minutes, until the onion is softened. Spoon into a wide casserole or earthenware dish, preferably one with a lid — if you don't have one of these, you can use a roasting tray and make a cover with foil. Add the lamb, potatoes, bay leaf and parsley, along with a few good glugs of olive oil. Season well with salt and pepper, and mix everything together, making sure there's a roughly even distribution of the ingredients in the dish.

Next into the pot are the halved tomatoes. Pop them on the top, and season with salt. Add the rice, pour in the hot stock or water, and cover, tightly, with a lid or kitchen foil.

Place in the oven and cook for 2½ hours, checking occasionally, basting and adding more stock if need be. At the end of the cooking time, the lamb should be meltingly soft and the potatoes should be perfectly cooked. If not, return the dish to the oven for a further 10–20 minutes with the lid in place.

When the lamb and potatoes are cooked, turn the oven up to 200°C/400°F/gas mark 6. Remove the lid or foil, sprinkle everything liberally with olive oil, and cook uncovered for a further 30–40 minutes, until the tomatoes are caramelized and the potatoes are golden.

Jamie Oliver
SPRING AND SUMMER
MINESTRONE

Nowadays, Chicago has the third largest Italian-American population in the United States, but when Fogg passed through there were apparently only forty-three Italian residents from Sicily and Italy's southern states. Jamie Oliver, an Englishman with an Italian 'Godfather', has made me this soup many a time, most memorably while visiting an island women's prison.

SERVES 4
PRISONERS

For the minestrone
Extra virgin olive oil
1 large red onion, finely chopped
3 cloves of garlic, peeled and
    finely sliced
200g/7oz small carrots,
    finely sliced
3 rashers of smoked streaky
    bacon, finely chopped
200g/7oz baby courgettes,
    finely sliced
1 large tomato, roughly chopped
A bunch of fresh flat-leaf parsley,
    roughly chopped, stalks and all
2 big handfuls of seasonal
    leaves, such as chard
    or cabbage, shredded
2 big handfuls of frozen peas
2 litres/3½ pints organic
    vegetable stock
150g/5oz baby farfalle pasta
Sea salt and freshly ground
    black pepper
2 big handfuls of soft round
    lettuce leaves
½ a head of chicory or
    radicchio, shredded
A few torn courgette flowers,
    if you can get them

Put a large pan on a medium heat and add a few lugs of good olive oil, the onion, garlic, carrots and bacon. Stir well and cook for 5 minutes, then add the courgettes and cook for 3–4 minutes, until soft.

Add the tomato, parsley, greens and peas, then pour in your stock and bring to the boil. Once boiling, add the mini pasta and a pinch of salt and pepper. Bring to the boil, then turn down the heat and simmer for 10 minutes.

While your soup is brewing, make the pesto. Take a large bunch of fresh basil, a couple of garlic cloves, 40g of grated Parmesan cheese and 60g of pine nuts and pound them all together with a pestle and mortar, loosening the mixture with extra virgin olive oil.

Just before the soup is ready, stir in the lettuce, chicory or radicchio and courgette flowers, if using. Check the seasoning, add salt and pepper if necessary, and serve each helping of soup with a good dollop of pesto, a drizzle of olive oil and a scattering of the little basil leaves.

NEW YORK
LONG ISLAND
ATLANTIC
OCEAN
UNITED STATES OF AMERICA
NEW YORK, N.Y.
EXCHANGE
No. 2471
M.G. TO
Railway and Steamship Ticket Office
No. 4 MONTGOMERY AVE.
P. O. Box 2487 San Francisco, Cal.
REGISTERED

NEW YORK

'At last the Hudson came into view;
and at a quarter-past eleven on the evening
of the 11th, the train stopped in the station
on the right bank of the river, before the very
pier of the Cunard Line. *The China*, for
Liverpool, had started three-quarters
of an hour before!'

Jamie Oliver
WALDORF SALAD JAMIE'S WAY

This speciality dish was created by Oscar Tschirky, *maître d'hotel* of the Waldorf Hotel in NYC in the 1890s. 'Oscar of the Waldorf' is also said to have developed Eggs Benedict (see overleaf) and popularized Thousand Island Dressing. As Cole Porter sang, 'You're the top! You're a Waldorf salad.' This is a Big Apple classic from Jamie Oliver.

SERVES 4

4 large handfuls of interesting lettuce leaves (frisée, romaine, endive, rocket, watercress or anything else you fancy), washed and spun dry

2 large handfuls of seedless or seeded green or red grapes, halved

3 medium sticks of celery, trimmed

2 large handfuls of walnuts, roughly crumbled

A small bunch of fresh flat-leaf parsley

150g/5oz blue cheese, such as dolcelatte

For the dressing

1 heaped teaspoon Dijon mustard

2 tablespoons white or red wine vinegar

6 tablespoons extra virgin olive oil

1 heaped tablespoon natural yoghurt

Sea salt and freshly ground black pepper

In a large bowl, toss together your leaves and your grapes. Use a speed-peeler to remove the stringy bits from the outside of your celery, then finely slice it on an angle and toss it in with the leaves and grapes.

Put a dry pan over a medium heat. Add the walnuts and give them a light toasting, shaking the pan every 25 seconds or so. Discard the tougher ends of your parsley stalks, and finely chop the rest of the stalks. Put these to one side, then chop the leaves and add to your salad bowl.

Make the salad dressing in a clean jam jar. Put the chopped parsley stalks into the jar with your mustard and vinegar, add three times as much extra virgin olive oil, then the yoghurt and finally a good pinch of salt and pepper. Screw the lid on tightly and shake it up nice and vigorously.

Drizzle enough dressing into the bowl to cover your leaves and scatter the walnuts over the top. Toss the salad gently.

Finally, using a knife, pare off little knobs of blue cheese and throw them into the salad bowl until you've a good amount – you don't want to be scrabbling around the bowl to find a cheesy nibble, but nor do you want to overwhelm your mouth.

You could garnish your Waldorf with matchsticks of crispy red apple or pear, depending on season.

Finally: drizzle with a little good olive oil and serve.

April Bloomfield
OYSTERS ROCKEFELLER

Oysters Rockefeller was created in 1899 by a chap called Jules, son of the founder of Antoine's restaurant in New Orleans, and named after John D. Rockefeller, then America's richest man, because of its rich sauce. Antoine Alciatore fled to New Orleans after two frustrating years trying to open restaurants in New York. But April Bloomfield, my good chum from the Midlands, has made New York her home. Her Spotted Pig, in the city's Greenwich Village, is one of my top culinary watering holes in the world. This is her Oysters Rockefeller.

SERVES 1

700g/1½lb spinach
10g/½oz butter
2 tablespoons diced shallots
¾ teaspoon finely
  chopped garlic
¾ teaspoon plain flour
100ml/4fl oz double cream
Coarse sea salt
Grated zest of ½ a lemon
1 tablespoon grated
  Parmesan cheese
2–3 dried pequin chillies,
  chopped
2 teaspoons lemon juice
12 large Island Creek oysters
  (or any large briny oysters)

For the topping
50g/2oz fresh breadcrumbs
25g/1oz grated Parmesan
  cheese
2 knobs of soft lemon butter

Blanch the spinach in salted boiling water, then drain and refresh in ice-cold water. Carefully press all the water out of the spinach, using a clean tea towel. This should yield about 125g/4½oz, half a cup or so, of cooked spinach. Chop the spinach nice and fine and set aside.

Melt the butter in a small pan, then add the shallots and garlic and cook gently until softened. Add the flour and cook until golden brown. Add the cream and ¼ teaspoon of sea salt and cook over a low heat for 20 minutes. Take the pan off the heat and add the lemon zest.

Put the spinach into a bowl, add the cream mixture and gently mix together. Add the Parmesan, chilli, lemon juice and ½ teaspoon of sea salt. Check and add more seasoning if necessary.

Preheat your grill. Open the oysters and place them in their half shells in an ovenproof dish or grill pan.

Place approximately ¾ teaspoon of the spinach mixture on top of each oyster.

Sprinkle with breadcrumbs and Parmesan, dot with the butter, and place under the grill until golden brown.

David Loftus
CLASSIC EGGS BENEDICT

According to the classic legend, Eggs Benedict was invented in New York in the 1860s at Delmonico's restaurant in Manhattan to rejuvenate the decidedly bored palates of upper-crust regulars, Mr & Mrs Le Grand Benedict. The revisionist myth suggests that the dish was born when Lemuel Benedict, a Wall Street businessman, ordered toast, bacon, poached eggs and a jug of hollandaise as a hangover cure at the Waldorf Hotel in 1894. The *maître d'hotel* — one Oscar Tschirky of Waldorf Salad fame and previously the head waiter at Delmonico's — then added it to the menu. Either way, one bite of this soft pillow of poached egg and bacon and I'm set for the day.

SERVES 6

900ml/1½ pints water
60ml/2fl oz distilled
    white vinegar
½ teaspoon sea salt
6 large, free-range
    organic eggs
6 English muffins, halved
175g/6oz good bacon,
    thinly sliced
A handful of fresh
    chives, chopped

For a cheat's hollandaise
12 heaped teaspoons of a
    good quality mayonnaise
3 heaped teaspoon of
    Dijon mustard
90g of good freshly grated
    cheddar cheese
Lemon juice of 1½ lemons
Sea salt and black pepper

Preheat your grill. For your cheat's hollandaise, gently mix the mayonnaise, mustard, lemon juice and a wee splash of water in a small heat proof bowl over a simmering pan of water. Stir occasionally. When warmed and well mixed, add the cheddar and a pinch of salt and of pepper and stir gently until the cheese has melted into the sauce.

Meanwhile, get working on your eggs. Measure your water, vinegar and sea salt into a pan and heat to a simmer. Crack 3 eggs, carefully, into three separate small cups. One after the other, pour the eggs against the side of the pan so that they slide smoothly into the simmering water and vinegar. Cook each egg for about 3 minutes, so the yolk is still soft and the white is firm. Remove with a slotted spoon and place the pretty white dumpling of egg on some kitchen paper and keep warm. Repeat with the remaining 3 eggs.

Place the bacon under the grill for 3–4 minutes on one side and around 2 minutes on the other. Lightly toast your muffin halves under the grill, just a couple of minutes each side.

Put a muffin piece on each plate, dividing up half the bacon between them. Top each one with the remaining muffin half, the rest of the bacon, and a poached egg. Drape a few tablespoons of hollandaise sauce over the top, and sprinkle with freshly chopped chives.

Jamie Oliver
MAC AND CHEESE

This all-American classic dates back to the days of Thomas Jefferson. This is Jamie's fairly traditional take on the ultimate comfort food. We ate this in a little apartment we rented on the Lower East Side, feeling a little like the odd couple, though of course he's odder than me.

SERVES 6 HUNGRY NEW YORKERS

450g/1lb macaroni
50g/2oz unsalted butter, plus a little for greasing
1½ large onions, diced
2 cloves of garlic, crushed
3 tablespoons plain flour
950ml/1½ pints whole milk
2 teaspoons sea salt
1 teaspoon freshly ground black pepper
½ teaspoon ground nutmeg
1 teaspoon paprika
250g/9oz sharp Cheddar cheese, grated
2 plum tomatoes, sliced
25g/1oz breadcrumbs (mixed with a sprinkling of dried mixed herbs and a dash of sea salt)
Extra virgin olive oil
A small mixed bunch of fresh parsley, thyme and chives

Preheat your oven to 200°C/400°C/gas mark 6 and butter a baking dish of around 25cm across. Cook the macaroni in boiling salted water according to the packet instructions, then drain and set aside.

Melt the butter in a large pan over a medium heat. Add the onions and garlic and cook until they soften. Add the flour and whisk until the mixture turns light brown, then slowly add the milk, whisking as you go. Add the salt, pepper, nutmeg and paprika.

Reduce the heat to low, and keep stirring until the sauce thickens. When it does so, add the cheese a little at a time, continuing to stir until melted. Add the cooked macaroni to the pan, and – yes – stir until the pasta is thoroughly coated.

Remove from the heat and pour into your baking dish. Lay the sliced tomatoes on top, sprinkle with the flavoured breadcrumbs and drizzle with extra virgin olive oil. Place in the oven and bake until bubbling and golden brown – probably about 30 minutes. Sprinkle with the chopped herbs, and serve. Cheesy goodness.

Molly Wrigglesworth
BOURBON PECAN PIE

Our final New York dish is pecan pie, served in diners up and down this great city. Originally based on a 'transparent pie' — a pie with a glossy sweet filling made of brown sugar, molasses or maple syrup — it was probably invented by a native of New Orleans, having purchased a few handfuls of the southern nuts from an Algonquian Indian. 'Pecan' is Algonquian for 'hard nut to crack' — a little like our illustrious hero.

SERVES
AT LEAST 8

For the pastry
300g/11oz plain flour
2 tablespoons granulated
    sugar
1 teaspoon sea salt
175g/6oz unsalted butter,
    cut into 1cm/½ inch cubes
    and softened
3–4 tablespoons iced water

For the filling
3 large eggs
350g/12oz golden syrup
75g/3oz light brown sugar
40g/1½oz unsalted butter,
    melted and cooled
3 tablespoons Kentucky
    bourbon
1½ teaspoons vanilla extract
½ teaspoon ground cinnamon
450g/1lb pecans

First make the pastry dough. Sift the flour, sugar and salt into a medium-sized bowl. Add the softened butter and mix together (in a blender, with a fork or by hand) until fully, but coarsely, combined. Slowly add the iced water, bit by bit, stirring until the dough begins to firm up. Go on instinct here – add a little more water if the dough seems too dry. Cover with clingfilm and leave in the fridge for at least an hour.

Preheat the oven to 170°C/325°F/gas mark 3 and when the dough is ready, roll it out and press it into a loose-bottomed pie dish. Chill for 20 minutes in the fridge. Now, blind-bake in the hot oven placing baking beans on top of the pastry to keep it from rising. Remove the pastry from the oven after 15–20 minutes, or when the crust is golden. Set aside to cool and remove the baking beans.

Meanwhile, to make the filling, whisk together the eggs, corn syrup and brown sugar. Add the cooled melted butter and whisk until well mixed. Next whisk in the bourbon, vanilla and cinnamon, and stir in the pecans. Pour the filling into your pie shell and bake for about 20–25 minutes, until set. Keep checking the pie, as it's easy for it to burn in just a couple of minutes.

When cooked, place on a rack to cool before serving with whipped cream on the side.

THE ATLANTIC CROSSING

'The *Henrietta* passed the lighthouse which marks
the entrance of the Hudson, turned the point of
Sandy Hook, and put to sea. During the day she
skirted Long Island, passed Five Island, and
made her course rapidly eastward.'

SPEEDY SALADS
DINING

Andy Harris's

SPEEDY SALADS FOR ON-DECK DINING

After the stresses and strains of finding a ship to take our heroes on to London, let us consider a few easy salads for on-deck dining as the *Henrietta* steams out of New York's harbour under the command of 'Captain Speedy'. I've eaten so many of Andy Harris's delicious salads, most memorably upon the deck of an old sailing boat, watching the sun set over the rooftops of a nearby coastal town. They are never boring and are always different, always a delight.

POMEGRANATE AND RED ONION SALAD

Cut 2 ripe pomegranates in half, then use the back of a spoon to beat the seeds into a bowl. Peel and thinly slice 450g/1lb of red onions and add to the bowl. Mix well, and season with sea salt and freshly ground black pepper. Leave to stand for about 20 minutes, then drizzle with olive oil and serve.

GRATED CUCUMBER SALAD

Combine ¼ teaspoon of ground cumin and 1 teaspoon of sea salt in a small bowl. Peel and grate 1 small cucumber, then add it to a bowl with 3 tablespoons of extra-virgin olive oil and the juice of ½ a lemon. Mix well. Add a thinly sliced red onion, sprinkle with cumin salt and serve.

CAULIFLOWER AND OLIVE SALAD

Boil 600g/1lb 6oz of cauliflower florets in salted water till tender. Drain and put into a bowl with 100g/3½oz of pitted mixed olives. Add 1 teaspoon of ground coriander, 1 teaspoon of ground turmeric and ½ teaspoon of ground ginger and season with sea salt and freshly ground black pepper. Mix well, and drizzle with extra virgin olive oil and the juice of half a lemon.

RADISH AND ORANGE SALAD

Peel and segment 3 oranges, then trim and finely slice a bunch of radishes and 1 red onion. Put into a bowl and add 5 tablespoons of extra virgin olive oil. Mix well, and season generously with sea salt and a little black pepper.

BEETROOT AND PURSLANE SALAD

Cook 450g/1lb of beetroot in boiling salted water until tender, then drain, peel and chop roughly. Put into a bowl with 75g/3oz of purslane and season with sea salt and freshly ground black pepper. Mix well, and dress with 5 tablespoons of extra virgin olive oil and 1 tablespoon of white wine vinegar.

HERB SALAD WITH PRESERVED LEMON DRESSING

Make a dressing by combining 1 roughly chopped preserved lemon, 1 tablespoon za'atar spice mix (available from specialist delis and some supermarkets), 4 tablespoons of extra virgin olive oil and 2 tablespoons of cider vinegar in a bowl. Place 75g/3oz of lamb's lettuce in a serving bowl with 75g/3oz of mixed baby herbs. Just before serving, pour over the dressing and toss.

Sarah Tildesley's tip: tomatoes come in so many different shapes, sizes and colours. Try some new varieties and create joyful, playful salads that look like little stained glass windows.

Rosie Scott and Sir Johnny Scott
RUM FOR TIRED TRAVELLERS AND JOLLY SAILORS

On board the steamship *Henrietta*, Passepartout is on the friendliest of terms with the sailors, astonishing them with his acrobatic performances and no doubt concocting the most attractive sun-past-the yardarm snifters. Sir Johnny Scott, a modern-day Phileas Fogg, hasn't had a tipple for over twenty years, but as former brake man for the British bob-sleigh team, farmer of black-faced sheep on the Lammermuirs, Joint Master of the North Pennine Hunt, passionate supporter of country issues, and board member of The European Squirrel Institute, these nautical nectars are but droplets from his fountain of culinary knowledge: piratical tipples for landlubbers and sea-dogs alike.

HOT BUTTERED RUM
SERVES 1

Hot buttered rum, a true after-watch special, one to remove the chill from your bones, and warm the cockles.

To a generous measure of rum, add a dash of Angostura bitters. Melt a teaspoon of butter and add it to your liquor; then top it up with a tot of piping hot water. Drop in a star anise and a few cloves. Inhale first, then quaff with piratical abandon.

Tip: try adding a cinnamon stick, lemon and cloves; or some Breton cider, a cinnamon stick and a sprinkling of caster sugar.

SPICED RUM CIDER
SERVES 1

Pour a good glug of light rum into a tall glass and add a teaspoon of light brown sugar. Stir with a stick of cinnamon and inhale the spicy fragrance. Top up with delicious apple cider before kicking back, sipping slowly and dreaming of the high seas.

SEAFOOD WAYS

Andy Harris
SEAFOOD TWO WAYS

All this beautiful seawater, and we haven't cooked any seafood for a little while. Let's remedy that. Lovely Andy Harris cooked me these dishes on a rocky outcrop looking out over Elizabeth Bay in Sydney to remind me of times spent on the sailing boat *Thelginos* in the Peloponnese, hunting for elusive octopi. A simple seafood delight.

SERVES 4

500g/1lb 2oz large
   octopus tentacles
2 tablespoons red
   wine vinegar
500g/1lb 2oz salad
   potatoes, peeled
Sea salt and freshly
   ground black pepper
2 baby fennel bulbs,
   trimmed and sliced
A handful of pitted
   green olives
6 tablespoons extra
   virgin olive oil
Juice of ½ a lemon
2 tablespoons white
   wine vinegar

SERVES 4-6

250g/9oz tuna, cut into
   1cm/½ inch pieces
250g/9oz mackerel or sea bass,
   cut into 1 cm/½ inch pieces
2 tablespoons toasted nori
   seaweed, shredded
1 tablespoon grated
   fresh ginger
1 tablespoon toasted
   sesame seeds
1½ tablespoons soy sauce
½ tablespoon extra virgin
   olive oil
4 tablespoons fresh or
   rehydrated seaweed,
   or pickled samphire

OCTOPUS, POTATO AND OLIVE SALAD

To cook the octopus tentacles, place them in a large pan of water with the red wine vinegar. Bring to the boil and simmer for 40–60 minutes, or until tender. Cut into slices.

Cook the potatoes in boiling salted water and drain. Leaving some whole and halving others, put them into a bowl with the fennel and olives. Drizzle with the extra virgin olive oil, lemon juice and white wine vinegar. Season with salt and pepper and mix well. Add the octopus slices and serve immediately, while discussing octopus-catching opportunities over a glass of Chablis.

A GREAT STARTER: 'MIXED POKE'

The fish should be sashimi-grade from sustainable sources.

Mix all the ingredients together and leave to marinate in the fridge for 5 minutes. Easy. Serve with Swedish-style crispbreads.

Sir Johnny Scott
VICTORIAN TABLE MANNERS

Whether dining at the Reform Club or banqueting onboard a steam ship, Phileas Fogg would sit before a 'cover' or place setting, consisting of a service plate or 'charger' and a side plate with a crisply folded napkin. To the right of the service plate – from outside in – would be the oyster knife resting in the bowl of the soup spoon, the fish knife, meat knife and salad knife. To the left, working in, would be the fish, meat and salad forks. In front and to the right were glasses for water, sherry champagne and white wine; to the right a saltcellar, pepper caster. More cutlery, crockery and glasses would be added as the meal progressed. The rigid rules of Victorian society dictated the cutlery used for each course, and the manner in which they should be employed. It was the worst of solecisms to neglect the procedure.

Dinner began with a choice of two soups: a clear soup, such as a consommé, and a thick one, such as chestnut. The soup spoon was swept away from the diner, never towards. Next was the fish course: Turbot with Lobster Sauce, or Poached Salmon Mousseline. Only the fish fork could be used. Next came the entrées, which might include Salmi of Widgeon with mushroom sauce. These were 'made' dishes, again to be eaten with the fork only.

Relevés or 'removes' followed the *entrées*. These were more substantial dishes, such as rolled, braised Sirloin of Beef à la Godard with mushrooms, truffles and sliced sweetbreads in a thick brown sauce. Depending on the time of year, Stuffed Hare à la d'Orleans with brown sauce, vinegar, hard-boiled egg white, anchovies, capers and gherkins, or Pheasant and Mushrooms à la Bohémienne might also have graced Fogg's plate.

These dishes were usually served with elaborately cooked vegetables: cardoons and Jerusalem artichokes, boiled and sliced à la Alphonse, dressed with peas in white sauce, garnished with little rolls of fried bacon and watercress, or pureed with cream and parmesan cheese.

Roasts were next on the menu and were invariably fowl of some sort: squab, pigeons, quail and – during the season – plover, snipe, grouse, partridge, pheasant, woodcock or wild duck. Game or poultry should not be eaten with fingers but with knife and fork.

Roasts might be followed by a palate cleanser, perhaps tomato sorbet, before the heavy, rich, 'entremets' or desserts. Jellies, blancmanges, ice puddings and sweet pastries were always eaten with a fork. Fruit tarts were the exception, where a dessert spoon could be used. Finally, savoury entremets, such as devilled anchovies, were brought to the table, followed by cheese, biscuits and fruit. At a formal dinner party, coffee and petit fours were served to the ladies in the drawing room, whilst the gentlemen remained at table for port, brandy, liqueurs and cigars.

Above all, Victorian diners had to remember to leave a morsel on the plate at the end of each interminable course. A clean plate indicated greed, or implied that the host's hospitality was wanting. Indeed, it was *de rigueur* 'to leave something for the "Duke"', since Manners was the family name of the Dukes of Rutland.

Jamie Oliver
JEWISH PENICILLIN

Fogg and his party have nine days in which to cross the 3,000 miles of ocean that lie between New York's harbour and Liverpool's docks, and then make their way to London. Heading north in December, with 'frequent fogs and heavy gales', these sharp conditions call for legendary Jewish mother's chicken soup. This is soup for the long haul.

SERVES 10–12
HUNGRY SAILORS

1 × 2.5kg/5½lb free-range or organic chicken

2 medium onions, peeled and roughly chopped

3 carrots, peeled and roughly chopped

3 sticks of celery, trimmed and roughly chopped

4 cloves of garlic, peeled

4 fresh bay leaves

A few sprigs of fresh thyme

Sea salt and freshly ground black pepper

2 handfuls of Jewish fine egg noodles, or spaghetti, broken into short bits

A small bunch of fresh flat-leaf parsley, roughly chopped

A small bunch of fresh dill, roughly chopped

Rinse your chicken in cold water, pat it dry with kitchen paper and place in a large cooking pot. Cover with cold water to reach about 8–10cm/3–4 inches above the chicken. Bring to the boil, then turn the heat down and simmer for 30 minutes. Using a spoon, skim off and discard the residue that will have gathered in a foamy layer on the top.

Add the chopped vegetables, cloves of garlic, bay leaves and thyme and season with a good pinch of salt. Bring everything back to the boil, then turn the heat down and leave to simmer for 1 hour more. Keep on skimming the scummy froth with a spoon.

When your soup is ready transfer the chicken to a roasting pan. Leave to cool, uncovered, for a few minutes. Remove the soup pot from the stove and, very carefully, strain everything through a large sieve, collecting the clear broth in a vessel large enough to contain its volume. When you've strained the vegetables from the liquid, pour the broth back into the pan and salvage all the nicest-looking vegetable chunks and drop them back into the soup.

Bring the soup back to the boil. When it's reached a steady roll, cover the pan with a lid, reduce the heat underneath and simmer gently. After 10 minutes, add your noodles or spaghetti to the pan. Replace the lid and simmer for a further 10 minutes, until the noodles are cooked.

Shred the meat, removing any trace of skin and bone, and add it to the soup along with the chopped herbs. Warm through for a few minutes, then season with salt and pepper and serve.

The Hart Brothers
SEAFOOD À LA HART

Seven hundred and seven miles from Liverpool, the *Henrietta* is running out of coal.
Fogg is a desperate man and there's mutiny ahoy. Piratical seafood dishes, then,
from the Spanish Main men, Eddie and Sam Hart. Me Harties.

SERVES 4 PICADORS AS A STARTER

400g/14oz fresh clams, cleaned
50g/2oz Serrano ham, cut
   into 5mm/¼ inch cubes
½ an onion, peeled and
   finely chopped
2 cloves of garlic, peeled
   and finely chopped
125ml/4½fl oz fino or
   manzanilla sherry
A small handful of fresh
   flat-leaf parsley, chopped
Extra virgin olive oil

CLAMS WITH SHERRY AND HAM

Check over the clams, discarding any that are open
and don't close when tapped. Heat a large, heavy-
based pan until very hot – and make sure you maintain
this heat throughout the cooking. Throw in the ham
and fry, stirring, for 1 minute. Add the onion and
garlic and cook for another minute, stirring constantly.
Add the clams and the sherry, cover with a tight-
fitting lid and cook over a high heat for 2 minutes,
or until the shells have steamed open.

   Remove from the heat. Pick out and discard any
unopened clams. Scatter with chopped parsley and
a good drizzle of olive oil and serve with strong
bread for mopping up the juices.

SERVES 4

1kg/2lb 2oz fresh
   mussels, cleaned
25ml/1fl oz extra virgin
   olive oil
1 tablespoon sherry vinegar
A small handful of fresh
   flat-leaf parsley,
   roughly chopped
A few small sprigs of
   fresh thyme
Sea salt and freshly
   ground black pepper

MUSSELS VINAIGRETTE

Pick over the mussels and discard any that are
open and that don't close when tapped. Put a large,
heavy-based frying pan on a high heat. When the
pan is piping hot and almost smoking, add the
mussels with 25ml/1fl oz of water. Cover with a
tight-fitting lid and cook for about 2 minutes, until
the mussels have opened. Remove the pan from
the heat. Pick through the mussels, discarding any
that have not opened. Add the extra virgin olive oil,
sherry vinegar and herbs, season with salt and
pepper, and toss together well in the pan. Serve
immediately in warmed bowls.

Rose Gray and Ruth Rogers
ZUPPA ALLA VONGOLE À LA RIVER CAFÉ

From my ultimate heroine, Rose Gray, this recipe is more like a quick lunchtime
fish stew than a soup. It's a dish full of steaming clams from the high seas.

SERVES 6

2kg/4½lb small clams,
   washed
Extra virgin olive oil
3 cloves of garlic, peeled
   and finely chopped
2 dried red chillies,
   crumbled
3 tablespoons chopped
   fresh flat-leaf parsley
1 bottle of dry white
   Italian wine
12 small slices of
   sourdough bread

Check over the clams, discarding any that are
already open and don't close when tapped. Heat
2 tablespoons of olive oil in a thick-bottomed pan,
add the garlic, chillies, and half the parsley and
cook for a few minutes.

Add the wine, bring to the boil and cook for a
minute, then add the clams. Stir well, coating the
clams in the hot wine, then cover and cook over
a high heat for 2–3 minutes. Discard any clams
that remain closed.

Toast or grill your slices of bread and arrange
them around the edge of a round or oval dish.
With a slotted spoon, remove the clams from the
pan and put them into the bottom of the dish.
Boil the liquid in the pan for a few minutes, until
reduced, then pour it over the clams. Sprinkle
with the remaining parsley and drizzle with
plenty of extra virgin olive oil.

David Loftus
OMELETTE ARNOLD BENNETT

As the *Henrietta* sails on through unwelcoming North Atlantic waters, interiors, bunks, masts, and rafts are all thrown into the steamer's furnace, the crew lost in 'a perfect rage for demolition' in an effort to keep on schedule. Amid all this wreckage and destruction, I think it's time we celebrated the miraculous oily fishies that surround us. This mackerel recipe was created in the 1920s by the chefs at the Savoy Hotel, London, for author and critic Arnold Bennett, who was staying there while writing his novel *Imperial Palace*. As Fogg heads towards home, here is a true British classic that remains on the Savoy's menu to this day.

SERVES 2

25g/1oz butter
¼ of a small onion, finely chopped
100g/3½oz smoked mackerel fillet
1 bay leaf
A few fresh thyme leaves
A pinch of ground nutmeg
3 free-range eggs, beaten
Salt and freshly ground black pepper
3 tablespoons double cream
1 tablespoon grated Parmesan cheese
1 tablespoon chopped fresh parsley
1 tablespoon extra virgin olive oil

Before you start, preheat your grill to hot. Melt half the butter in a frying pan and add the onion. After a few minutes, as the onion becomes soft, add the smoked mackerel, bay leaf, thyme, nutmeg and enough boiling water to cover the fish. Cover with a lid, turn the heat down, and poach for 5 or 6 minutes, until the mackerel has cooked through. Remove the fish from the pan using a fork, and flake.

Clean your frying pan. Season the eggs with salt and pepper, then melt the remaining butter and add the beaten eggs. Cook for about 3 minutes, using a spatula to move the uncooked egg around until it begins to set. Add the flakes of fish, the cream and the grated Parmesan and pop the frying pan under a hot grill for a few minutes to brown the top of the omelette. Slide it on to a hot serving plate, sprinkle with the parsley and drizzle with extra virgin olive oil.

David Loftus
HERRINGS WITH POTATO À LA SUÉDOISE

The cold countries of the North Atlantic love their herrings, as we once did. They were barrel-salted, smoked, rollmopped, red-herringed and scoffed in their millions in days of old. This is just one way to enjoy these abundant little blighters.

SERVES 4 HUNGRY LOFTUSES

2 large red onions, sliced into thin rings
300g/11oz herring fillets
Groundnut oil
500g/1lb 2oz new potatoes
Fresh dill leaves, dill flowers, sliced chives or spring onions to garnish

For the vinaigrette
2 tablespoons red wine vinegar
Sea salt and freshly ground black pepper
3 tablespoons groundnut oil

A day before eating, start marinating the herrings. Pour the onions and the herring rings. Layer the herrings and sliced onions in a dish and pour in enough oil to cover. Cover the dish with clingfilm and refrigerate for 24 hours.

The following day, wash the potatoes and cook them, still in their skins, in boiling salted water until tender. Strain and set aside to cool down a bit while you prepare your vinaigrette. In a clean jam jar, combine the vinegar, salt, pepper and oil, and shake vigorously until well mixed. When the potatoes are cool enough to handle, slice them into rounds. Arrange in a serving dish and pour over the vinaigrette. Serve with the herrings and a smattering of pretty fresh dill leaves – dill flowers are even better, if you can find them. Chives or sliced spring onions also work well.

GREAT BRITAIN: THE END OF THE JOURNEY

'Phileas Fogg had only twenty-four hours
more in which to get to London…'

Irish Kate McCullough
MUSSELS IN GUINNESS

At last, Fogg has arrived on the Irish coast and is counting on gaining twelve hours by travelling with the mail from Dublin to Liverpool. Instead of arriving at Liverpool the next evening on the *Henrietta*, he plans to be there by noon, bundled among the parcels and envelopes. But we've time enough for a dash of 'the black stuff' before Fogg sets off for Great British shores.

SERVES 2 HEARTY IRISHMEN

A knob of butter
1 shallot, finely chopped
2 cloves of garlic, finely chopped
2 rashers of smoked streaky bacon, finely chopped
A small bunch of fresh thyme, leaves picked and chopped
A small bunch of flat-leaf parsley, leaves picked and chopped
1 bay leaf
Sea salt and freshly ground black pepper
1kg/2lb 2oz mussels, cleaned
250ml/9fl oz Guinness
50ml/2fl oz cream

Melt the butter in a large pan. Add the shallot, garlic and bacon and cook until the shallot is translucent and the bacon golden brown. Add half the thyme and parsley, the bay leaf and a pinch of salt and pepper.

Add the mussels to the pan, discarding any that are open and that will not close when you tap them, then pour in the Guinness. Bring to the boil, then turn down the heat and place a lid on the pan. Leave for 3–5 minutes, or until the mussels have steamed open. Remove the pan from the heat and discard any unopened mussels. Stir in the cream, and add the rest of the parsley and thyme. Taste the sauce and adjust the seasoning if necessary.

Serve immediately, with brown soda bread and salty butter.

Heston Blumenthal
WELSH RAREBIT OR RABBIT A LA HESTON

Like 'mock turtle soup', which has seen neither hide nor hare (!) of a turtle, Welsh Rabbit (as it was probably once called) has never been anywhere near a bunny. Now, as Fogg and his companions pass Wales on their journey towards Liverpool with the mail, it seems the perfect cheesy comfort food for an uncomfortable few hours. It's a sacred snack — but you can trust Heston Blumenthal to bring a little touch of magic to a classic.

SERVES 4-6

50g/2oz unsalted butter
50g/2oz plain flour
250ml/9fl oz Abbot or
  other strong ale
250g/9oz strong Cheddar
  cheese, grated
1 tablespoon Worcestershire
  sauce
½ tablespoon English mustard
1 teaspoon wholegrain mustard
1 egg yolk
Salt and freshly ground
  black pepper
1 bottle of medium dry
  white wine
10 cloves of garlic, peeled
  and crushed
1 sprig of fresh rosemary
1 sprig of fresh thyme
1 sprig of fresh tarragon
1 teaspoon black peppercorns
A bottle of good-quality white
  wine vinegar
A loaf of good sourdough bread
A sprinkle of fleurs de sel

On a low heat, melt the butter and stir in the flour to make a roux. Heat the ale, but do not let it boil, and add it to the mix, stirring gently and constantly over a low heat.

Melt the cheese in a bowl placed over a pan of boiling water. When melted, pour into the mixture. Stir once to amalgamate, then remove from the heat.

Add the Worcestershire sauce, both mustards, the egg yolk, salt and pepper, then transfer to a food processor and blitz until the rarebit mixture has formed an emulsion. Transfer to a bowl, allow to cool, then refrigerate.

For the accompanying vinegar, put the wine into a stainless steel pan over the heat and bring to the boil. Add the garlic, herbs and peppercorns and boil rapidly for 3–4 minutes. Take off the heat and strain through a fine sieve. When the liquid has cooled down, add 25ml/1fl oz of white wine vinegar to every 100ml/4fl oz of the wine mixture and set aside.

Heat a chargrill, or preheat your oven to 225°C/425°F/gas mark 7. Slice your sourdough about 2.5cm/1 inch thick – you will probably want 1 or 2 slices per person, depending on appetites. Brush both sides of each slice with melted butter, and chargrill or toast in the oven for 5 minutes.

Take your Welsh rarebit mixture out of the fridge and melt 40–50g per slice in a small pan. Put your sourdough slices on a baking tray and pour over the rarebit mixture. Cook in the oven for 4–5 minutes, until golden brown.

Sprinkle a few grains of fleurs de sel on top, and serve with the garlicky vinegar on the side, preferably café style in a vinegar shaker.

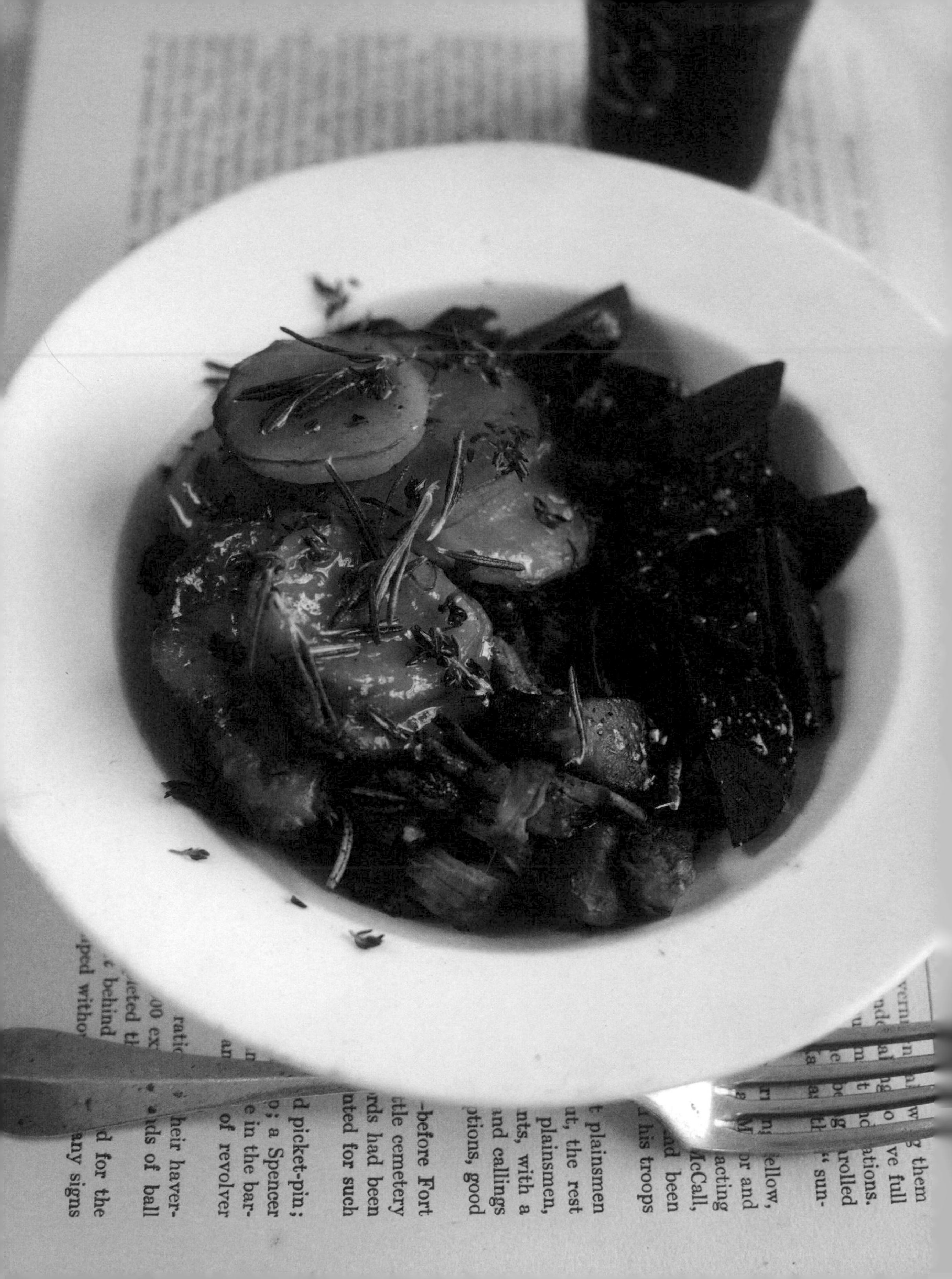

SCOUSE
HOT POT

Rosie Scott
SCOUSE HOT POT

No sooner has Fogg landed at Liverpool Pier than he is marched off by the police in a case of mistaken identity. He is just six hours from London. As we await news of his fate on the perishing dockside, I feel the need for a stew. Scouse: originally called Labskause, then shortened to Skause, then anglicized to Scouse. The lovely Rosie Scott used to cook this for me as an alternative to flu-busting chicken soup. It's an equally heart-warming tonic for a good night's sleep.

SERVES 6 HUNGRY SCOUSERS

Olive oil
900kg/2lb neck of lamb,
    trimmed of fat, cubed
450g/1lb stewing steak,
    fat removed and cubed
3 onions, peeled and sliced
900kg/2lb potatoes, peeled
    and sliced
900kg/2lb mixed carrot,
    swede and parsnip, cubed
1 tablespoon fresh thyme,
    chopped
1 tablespoon fresh
    rosemary, chopped
1½ litres/2½ pints beef stock
Salt and freshly ground
    black pepper
Worcestershire sauce

Preheat the oven to 170°C/325°F/gas mark 3. Heat a little olive oil in a heavy-based pan or casserole dish. When it's hot, add the lamb and beef cubes to brown and seal, turning often. As the meats begin to brown, add the onion. Carry on cooking and stirring for about 5 minutes.

Now add the rest of the vegetables and the herbs, and pour the beef stock into the pan to cover the contents. Place a lid on top, then put the lot into the oven for 2½–3 hours. When the casserole is ready, taste and season with salt, pepper and a dash of Worcestershire sauce.

Traditionally, this would be served with pickled beetroot or red cabbage and plates of thickly buttered white bread for mopping up.

LONDON : HOME AGAIN

'A great crowd was collected in Pall Mall
and the neighbouring streets on Saturday
evening; it seemed like a multitude of
brokers permanently established around
the Reform Club. Circulation was impeded,
and everywhere disputes, discussions,
and financial transactions were going on.
The police had great difficulty in keeping
back the crowd, and as the hour when
Phileas Fogg was due approached, the
excitement rose to its highest pitch.'

Danyel Couet
PAUPER'S TOAST WITH CHOCOLATE

Fogg makes it out of jail free, and catches the express train for London. The train steams into town but they are five minutes too late! Dismay! Ruination!... Consolatory breakfast, anyone? Fogg himself asks to be excused, but this 'toast-driven breakfast' has revived my sunken spirits several times. This recipe comes courtesy of the moustachioed Danyel Couet, *bon vivant* extraordinaire, great chum, and provider of the best picnics in Paris, the best fine dining in Stockholm and the best hangover cures in London. Why does hot buttered toast always taste so much better when toasted and buttered by someone else?

SERVES 2-4

4 slices of sourdough bread
Butter, for the bread
Caster sugar
Olive oil, for frying

For the chocolate cream
200g double cream
1 tablespoon olive oil
200g dark chocolate,
    broken into small pieces
½ teaspoon sea salt

Warm the cream and the olive oil in a pan. Take it off the heat as soon as the cream and oil come to the boil. Add the chocolate and stir until the cream is smooth. Stir in the sea salt and let the mixture sit for at least 1 hour.

Butter both sides of the bread slices and dip them in the sugar. Heat some olive oil in a frying pan and fry the slices on both sides until golden. Let them sit at room temperature for 5 minutes, then serve with the chocolate cream spread thickly.

Jamie Oliver
JAMIE'S KEDGEREE

Though Fogg is too disappointed to eat breakfast, it's got to be kedgeree for me. Smoky, creamy, fragrant and filling, it is believed that the recipe was taken to India by Scottish soldiers serving during the British Raj, where it was adopted as part of the local cuisine. Made popular as a start to the day by the Victorians, it is not to be forgotten at lunchtime or when you want a little late-night something-or-other.

SERVES 4 BREAKFASTING TRAVELLERS

2 large free-range eggs
700g/1½lb undyed smoked haddock fillets, pin-boned
2 fresh bay leaves
175g/6oz long-grain or basmati rice
Sea salt
110g/4oz pure butter ghee
A thumb-size piece of fresh ginger, peeled and grated
1 medium onion or 1 bunch of spring onions, finely chopped
1 clove of garlic, finely chopped
2 heaped teaspoons curry powder
1 tablespoon mustard seeds
2 tomatoes, seeded and finely chopped
Juice of 2 lemons
2 handfuls of fresh coriander, leaves picked and chopped
A small pot of natural yoghurt
1 fresh red chilli, finely chopped (optional)

Boil the eggs for 10 minutes, then leave them under cold running water for a couple of minutes to cool them down and prevent the yolks discolouring.

Place the fish and bay leaves in a shallow pan and add enough water to just cover them. Turn on the heat, gently bring to the boil, then cover the pan and simmer for about 5 minutes, until the fish is cooked through. Remove it from the pan and set aside to cool.

Meanwhile, cook the rice in boiling salted water for about 10 minutes, until tender. Drain and refresh in cold water, then drain again and leave covered in the fridge until needed.

By now your fish will be cool enough for you to remove the skin and gently flake the tender flesh into a bowl. Set aside.

Melt the butter ghee in a pan over a low heat, and add the ginger, onion and garlic. Soften for about 5 minutes, then add the curry powder and mustard seeds. Cook for a further few minutes, then add the chopped tomatoes and lemon juice.

Now, shell and quarter the hard-boiled eggs. Take your fish and rice, and add them to the pan of softened and spiced ingredients. Gently heat through. Finally, add the eggs and all but a teaspoon or two of the chopped coriander. Stir together gently, and pile the glistening kedgeree into a warm serving dish.

Mix the rest of the coriander into the yoghurt and add one finely chopped red chilli. Pour the yoghurt mixture into a small bowl and serve alongside the kedgeree, with a teaspoon for dolloping. Cool, clean, warm, spicy… It always hits the spot.

A WINTER WEDDING AND A RETURN TO THE REFORM CLUB

Back home in London after a very long journey, our weary travellers believe that all is lost and sink into their chairs, exhausted. Aouda asks our woebegone hero, 'what will become of you, Mr Fogg?' Downtrodden and disappointed, he replies, 'I have need of nothing'. At which, Aouda seizes his hand and makes an excellent suggestion:

'Do you wish at once a kinswoman and friend? Will you have me for your wife?' Mr Fogg, at this, rose in turn. There was an unwonted light in his eyes, and slight trembling of his lips. Aouda looked into his face. The sincerity, rectitude, firmness and sweetness of this soft glance of a noble woman, who could dare all to save him to whom she owed all, at first astonished, then penetrated him. He shut his eyes for an instant, as if to avoid her look. When he opened them again, 'I love you!' he said, simply. 'Yes, by all that is holiest, I love you, and I am entirely yours!'

Aouda's very romantic proposal marks a change of fortune. Things immediately start to look up for our gentleman voyager and his companions – as surely they always would. It transpires that there has been an uncharacteristic miscalculation, for in circumnavigating along an eastward route, Fogg and his friends actually gained a day! Fogg is in a cab faster than you can say 'Home, James,' and at the Reform Club as quick as lightning for a dashing and triumphant return.

At the fifty-seventh second the door of the saloon opened; and the pendulum had not beat the sixtieth second when Phileas Fogg appeared, followed by an excited crowd who had forced their way through the club doors, and in his calm voice, said, 'Here I am, gentlemen!'

Fogg has made it around the world in eighty days. He has won his wager!

Giuseppe Cipriani
BELLINI COCKTAIL

And so, the wager is won and the illustrious Phileas Fogg and his dear Aouda will be swapping the hurly burly of cross-continent travel for the comforts of the matrimonial bed. Our celebratory cocktail of choice? The Bellini, memorably quaffed with my chums Mr Harris and Arrigo Cipriani in Harry's Bar in Venice. Arrigo's father was the great Giuseppe Cipriani, who invented the drink in the very same bar having been bewitched by the pinkish glow emitted by the dying sun in his favourite painting by the fifteenth-century artist Giaranni Bellini. Drink slowly and sigh contentedly…

SERVES 2

2 ripe peaches, peeled, quartered and stone removed
chilled champagne or sparkling wine
2 chilled glasses

Put the peaches into a blender and purée until smooth. Divide the purée between the chilled glasses and then slowly top up with the champagne or sparkling wine, stirring as you pour. Serve these fragrant, fizzy masterpieces straight away.

Georgie Socratous
ELDERFLOWER AND GOOSEBERRY CAKE

Phileas Fogg's journey around the world has taken him eighty days, carried by steamships, railway carriages, yachts, trading vessels, sledges and elephants. His true prize is the love and companionship of his beloved Aouda. Our final recipe? A beautiful cake for a special occasion.

SERVES 8-10

275g/10oz unsalted butter,
    at room temperature
275g/10oz caster sugar
150g/5oz ground almonds
100ml/4fl oz elderflower
    cordial
5 large eggs
175g/6oz self-raising
    flour, sifted
350g/12oz gooseberry compote

For the frosting
500g/1lb 2oz icing sugar, sieved
125g/4½oz unsalted butter
300g/11oz cream cheese
55ml/2fl oz elderflower cordial

To serve
Decorate with fresh flowers;
if in season, with washed
elderflowers. Serve with
a flourish and a glass of
champagne

Preheat the oven to 180°C/350°F/gas mark 4, and grease and line two 23cm/9 inch round cake tins.

Cream the butter and sugar together until pale and fluffy, then mix in the ground almonds and half the elderflower cordial.

Gradually add the eggs, one at a time, then gently fold in the flour using a metal spoon. Divide the mixture between the two tins and bake in the oven for about 35–40 minutes, until a metal skewer comes out clean.

While the cakes are still hot and in the tin, pierce holes in the top of each one with a fine skewer or fork, and drizzle with the remaining elderflower cordial.

Leave the cakes to cool in the tins for 5 minutes, then remove and place on a rack. When they are cool, slice each cake in half horizontally, giving you 4 layers.

To make the frosting, cream together the icing sugar and the butter. When completely mixed, beat in the cream cheese for around 3–4 minutes until smooth. If you beat the mixture for too long, it will become runny. Lastly mix in the cordial and set aside.

Place the bottom half of one of the cakes on a cake stand or board. Spread a thin layer of the frosting over the surface, followed by a third of the gooseberry compote. Now place another round of cake on top, and spread with a layer of frosting and compote. Repeat with the next cake round, top that with a final layer of frosting and compote, then place the fourth round on top and cover the entire cake with frosting. If you like a smooth finish, dip a palette knife into hot water to smooth out the edges or use a large spoon to coat the sides and make little snowy peaks.

FAREWELL

Around the world in eighty days: the bet is won
and from the depths of despair come love, romance
and everlasting friendships. My eighty dishes not only
follow the route of our intrepid hero's voyage, but also
relate to my own personal journey. In *Around the World
in 80 Days*, we grow to realize – along with Fogg – that
in travel, as in life, you can plan all you like, but you
shall never beat fate, you'll never be able to predict the
future and, possibly most wonderfully of all, that there's
a whole lot to be gained by losing track of time.
Let's raise a glass to travel and travelling companions;
to friends both absent and present; to sharing these
recipes and moments with the ones you love; to filling
scrapbooks with recipes and cuttings like our
grandparents did; to keeping diaries and sketch
books; and – most of all – to embracing life.

And I raise a personal glass to my twin brother Johnny,

David Loftus

JULES VERNE

Born in February 1828, the young Jules Verne lived with his family on the Île Feydeau, a small rocky island in the Loire. The open water surrounding his home was an imaginative boy's dream and he spent hours watching the comings and goings at the quayside, turning them into tales of the high seas. After failed attempts at stowing away to travel the blue yonder, it was agreed that the young Jules should join a chum in Paris and he soon found himself immersed in the arty salons of the city. He decided that his future would certainly be that of a writer... Despite all this gay abandon, it was a hard time to live in the capital. Paris was falling to the Prussians and its people had suffered years of siege, hunger and heavy taxes. But Verne was to conjure up the perfect antidote for these troubled times. Drinking in a

Parisian café, he spotted a travel advertisement suggesting that it might be possible to circumnavigate the globe in just eighty days – the beginnings of a story. As Verne later explained: 'I have a great many scientific odds and ends in my head. It immediately struck me that I could profit by a difference in the meridian and make my traveller gain or lose a day in his journey. There was my denouement ready found.' In less than two weeks, Verne had crafted an outline for his tale, offering it to Parisian newspaper *Le Temps* for publication in installments. *Around the World in 80 Days* would become a hugely successful literary serial. Fogg's wager at the Reform Club caused such a sensation amongst *Le Temps*' readers that they too began to bet on the odds that Verne's hero would complete his journey in the given eighty days.

ALEXIS SOYER

Born in France in 1810, Alexis Benoit Soyer moved to England and in 1837 took the position of *chef de cuisine* at London's Reform Club. He was a hugely creative chef and his kitchens became so famous that they were open for conducted tours. But it wasn't just his food that caused a stir. During the Irish Potato Famine, Soyer travelled to Dublin to set up the first ever soup kitchen; by the early 1850s, he was touring the country to promote his 'magic stove' and recipe books; and in 1855, Soyer travelled to the battlefields of the Crimea with cooking facilities specially designed to help alleviate the horrific conditions faced by British soldiers. A culinary innovator, as well as social philanthropist, many of Soyer's best-known dishes are still on the Reform Club menu today. The most celebrated chef in Victorian England, Soyer could truly be called 'the father at modern cookery'.

JAMIE OLIVER

An Alexis Soyer of his generation: television personality, prolific writer of cookery books, restaurateur, philanthropist extraordinaire. Jamie's an Essex boy, born in 1975 to his publican parents, Sally and the rambunctious Trevor. Trev put young Jamie to work in The Cricketers at the Dickensian age of ten and Jamie the chef was born.

Told he had no hope by his careers master, it was under Italian Stallion mentor, Gennaro Contaldo, and later the wonderful Rose Gray at The River Café, that the boy Jamie matured into the Naked Chef. I shot his first portraits, for the cover of *The Times* Saturday magazine. We became firm friends and are now more like brothers. Today he employs thousands, and influences millions in hundreds of countries. Yet he is the same excitable, loveable scamp, generous godfather and extraordinary friend as always. I have so much to thank him for.

OUR CHEFS AND CONTRIBUTORS

PETE BEGG

Pete Begg works with Jamie Oliver in food development, having previously worked with him in kitchens as a chef. Pete has worked with David Loftus on all but one of Jamie's books: travelling, cooking and shooting photographs... as well as sharing many a 'Chablis o'clock' with David.

BELLA BELLISSIMA

Bella Crane – Bella Bellissima – is a fragrance designer and creator of the luxury perfume collection, Bella Bellissima. Bella has recently collaborated with Jamie Oliver to launch a range of fragrant products called 'Scent & Savour'.

RAVINDER BHOGAL

Ravinder Bhogal is an award-winning food writer, journalist, stylist and television personality. Her debut cookery book, *Cook in Boots*, was published to rave reviews both in the UK and America.

APRIL BLOOMFIELD

April Bloomfield is chef and co-owner of three restaurants: the Michelin-starred Spotted Pig; The Breslin Bar & Dining Room; and The John Dory Oyster Bar. April previously cooked at the River Café and did a stint at Alice Waters' Chez Panisse restaurant before opening The Spotted Pig.

HESTON BLUMENTHAL

Entirely self-taught, Heston Blumenthal is the most progressive chef of his generation. In 2004 he won the coveted three Michelin stars in near-record time for his restaurant The Fat Duck, which has twice been voted the Best Restaurant in the World. In 2006 he was awarded an OBE.

GUY BOTHAM

Guy Botham was born in England and left in his early twenties to travel. He drove across the Sahara, helped rebuild an Etruscan monastery, and ran a nightclub in Hong Kong. He made Hollywood, California, his home in 1995 and has produced several televisions shows and now runs a movie development company.

DOMENICA CATELLI

Domenica Catelli is a restaurateur, chef and educator – appearing on numerous American television food and news shows – as well as author of the cookbook *Mom-a-licious*. Domenica is the co-owner and chef of Catelli's restaurant in Geyserville, California.

CAESAR CARDINI

Caesar Cardini was a restaurateur, chef, and hotel owner. Born in Italy in 1896, he emmigrated to America after World War I and opened restaurants in Sacramento, San Diego, and Tijuana, where the famous Caesar Salad was invented.

GIUSEPPE CIPRIANI

Giuseppe Cipriani opened Harry's Bar in Venice in 1931 and since that time both the owner and the bar have become world renowned. Harry's Bar is the birthplace of the famous Bellini cocktail.

GENNARO CONTALDO

Gennaro Contaldo is a highly respected chef in London. Born in Minori on the Amalfi Coast, Gennaro's quintessentially Italian spirit and positive nature has made him a TV favourite and he is widely known as the Italian legend who taught Jamie Oliver all he knows about Italian cooking. He has written five cookbooks, most recently *Two Greedy Italians* with Antonio Carluccio.

DANYEL COUET

Danyel Couet is head chef at the Michelin-starred restaurant Fredsgatan 12 in Stockholm. He is also one of the restaurateurs behind Grill, Kungsholmen, Smak på Restaurangen, Fjällpuben, Brasserie Le Rouge, Fyran, Villa Godthem, Le Bar, Köttbaren and Miss Voon in Stockholm.

ROSE GRAY

Rose Gray, MBE, who died on 28 February 2010 aged 71, co founded the River Café restaurant in London with her business partner Ruth Rogers. Today, the River Café is one of the most respected restaurants in the world.

ANDY HARRIS

Andy Harris is the founding editor of *Jamie Magazine*, Jamie Oliver's food and travel magazine sold in over forty-five countries. His career spans magazines such as *Vogue Entertaining & Travel*, *Gourmet Traveller* and *Taste*, and he is the author of various food and travel books.

THE HART BROTHERS

Eddie and Sam Hart own several restaurants including Fino and Barrafina, as well as fronting the restaurant at Quo Vadis, the private members club. They have written several cookbooks on the art of Spanish cooking.

ANNA JONES

Anna Jones is a food writer, cook, eater, food stylist and a natural food lover. She is the author of *Hungry?*.

SYBIL KAPOOR

Sybil Kapoor is a chef, food writer and broadcaster who has won numerous awards for her innovative work. Sybil's books include *Citrus and Spice – A Year in Flavour*, *Taste*, and *Simply British*. Her latest project is www.sybilkapoor.com

RACHEL KHOO

Rachel Khoo studied pâtisserie in Paris at Le Cordon Bleu. She is a food creative who works on a variety of international culinary projects from food consulting and workshops, to culinary events and cookbooks. Her third cookbook, *The Little Paris Kitchen*, was published in April 2012 by Penguin.

ATUL KOCHHAR

Atul Kochhar is a twice Michelin-starred chef and the author of several renowned Indian cuisine cookbooks, such as *Indian Essence*. Atul is also featured in numerous television series, including *Atul's Spice Kitchen* and *Saturday Kitchen*

NIGELLA LAWSON

Nigella Lawson is the bestselling author of eight recipe books – *How to Eat; How to be a Domestic Goddess*; *Nigella Bites*; *Forever Summer*; *Feast*; *Nigella Express*; *Nigella Christmas* and *Kitchen* – which, together with her successful TV series, have made hers a household name around the world.

DEBBIE LOFTUS

Debbie Loftus was the illustrator and painter Debbie Lian Mason before she married David. She is the devoted mother of Pascale and Paros, is currently writing and illustrating a book about mushrooms aimed at youngsters, and is rarely seen without a sketch book or her Scottie, Pan.

DR LOFTUS

Dr Jean Loftus was born in County Durham. She met David's father, Eric, on her first visit to London. He proposed to her by slipping a note into her piano music as she played Chopin. They hadn't yet been introduced. She lived in the tower of Narworth Castle and in 'Romeo and Juliet' style he awaited her answer from below. A hugely popular and respected doctor, she retired after the death of her son and is currently researching her biography of Colonel Woodthorpe.

DEBORAH MADISON

The founding chef of San Francisco's Greens restaurant, Deborah Madison is a writer and cook, whose focus is on the vegetable side of the plate. Her eleven cookbooks include *Vegetarian Cooking for Everyone*; *Local Flavors* and *Seasonal Fruit Desserts*.

KATE MCCULLOUGH

Kate McCullough is a Dublin-born freelance food stylist and recipe writer living, cooking and eating in London, and missing the Guinness terribly.

TONY MILFORD, JR

Tony Milford, Jr lives in Window Rock, Arizona, in the capital of 'The Great Navajo Nation': 'My inspirations for cooking are my two lovely daughters, Ciara and Hyliah. As we keep the heritage of Dineh philosophy and respect the gifts of Mother Earth, which sustain us… her children, may each of you continue to always, "Walk in Beauty".'

DANIEL O'CONNELL

Daniel O'Connell was born in Ireland in 1849. After emmigrating to America, O'Connell forged a career as a writer and in 1872 co-founded the Bohemian Club in San Francisco, where he spent many an evening enjoying the food, drink and artistic entertainment. In 1891, he published *The Inner Man: Good Things to Eat and Drink and Where to Get Them*, advice for the epicurean who found himself in the San Francisco area.

JAMIE OLIVER

Jamie Oliver is one of the world's most respected and best-loved chefs. His books, TV series, restaurants and campaigns have inspired millions of people to cook and enjoy good food.

ADAM PERRY LANG

Adam Perry Lang is a chef, restaurateur and the cookbook author of *Serious Barbecue*, *BBQ25* and *Charred & Scruffed*.

RUTH ROGERS

Ruth Rogers, MBE came to fame co-founding the River Café with Rose Gray. Ruth continues to run the Michelin-starred restaurant, which counts April Bloomfield, Jamie Oliver and Hugh Fearnley-Whittingstall amongst its protégés.

SIR JOHNNY SCOTT

Sir Johnny Scott is an author, historian, broadcaster, columnist, countryside campaigner and farmer. He wrote and co-presented the BBC2 series *Clarissa and the Countryman* and contributes to a variety of magazines and periodicals on field sports, food, farming, travel, natural history and rural issues.

ROSIE SCOTT

The gorgeous Rosie is a food stylist, writer and maverick raconteur, brought up on the Lammermuirs and now living in London, where she entertains the Kensal Rise locals with her tales of Highland living, and her travels from Ladakh to Timbuktu. She is a rising star in the foody world.

GEORGIE SOCRATOUS

Georgie (Georgina) Socratous is a London-based food stylist and writer. Georgie has worked on numerous Jamie Oliver television series, including *Food Revolution, Jamie's 30 Minute Meals* and *Jamie's Great Britain*.

ALEXIS SOYER

Born in Meaux-en-Brie, France, in 1810, Alexis Soyer was *chef de cuisine* at the Reform Club in London from 1837 to 1850 and was considered the greatest chef of his era. He was also a philanthropist who organised food relief for the victims of the Irish Potato Famine and improved the diet and health of British soldiers during the Crimean War.

SARAH TILDESLEY

Sarah Tildesley is a food stylist who has had the joy to work on many exciting projects, from Jamie Oliver's beautiful television programmes, to making a life-size car out of cake for Skoda.

JAKE TILSON

Jake Tilson is an artist, graphic designer and author. His cookbook, *A Tale of 12 Kitchens,* won the Gourmand World Cookbook Award. The Tate recently acquired an artwork of his.

JODY VASSALLO

Jody Vassallo is a writer and food stylist who has written over thirty cookbooks. In 2003, she won the Gourmand World Food Media Award, Best Nutrition Series. For more about her visit jodyvassallo.com

ALICE WATERS

Alice Waters is the chef and proprietor of Chez Panisse in California. She is also the author of several cookbooks, including *The Art of Simple Food*. Alice Waters was awarded the French *Legion d'Honneur* in 2010.

MOLLY WRIGGLESWORTH

Mary Florence Wrigglesworth – Molly – was born in 1922 in Ryhope, County Durham. She has spent her life caring for other people – her parents, patients in local hospitals and last, but not least, the Loftus family, particularly the twins, David and John. An excellent and knowledgeable cook, her stir-fries, gravy and 'Auntie Molly's Apple Pie' are legendary.

MY THANK YOUS

My heartfelt thanks go to my family. To Debbie, my rock, for holding it all, and us, together through thick and thin. A talented artist, she has oft forgone her own ambitions to keep me on a straight path. You've put up with a lot, Debbie, and I love you. To Paros and Pascale, for being my *raison d'etre*, for giving me life and love. I love you more than words. To my dear mother, Dr Jean, for inspiring me with her mother's and her own cookery scrapbooks, and for marrying Eric, a true old-fashioned English Gentleman, whose charm affected us all and who instilled in us a strong moral code and a set of good manners whilst still allowing 'boys to be boys'. To my constantly-missed twin John, for sharing my life from conception until his early death. I am constantly in your shadow, I do hope you are proud on your cloud.

Thank you too to the delectable Sarah Norman at Atlantic Books, more used to Man Booker winners than scribblers like me, but patient and nurturing. I know I've given you some nail-biting moments, though you do have the prettiest hands. I hope your sleepless nights are now spent in peaceful slumber. To Toby and Margaret, my big bosses at Atlantic, for listening to Sarah Castleton when she suggested you publish the book, for having the faith and the commitment in a time of recession, for keeping going and seeing me through, with the occasional, but not too rough, kick in the seat of the pants. The Whispering Angels are on me. Thanks also to the rest of your talented crew, especially Alan Craig, Richard Evans, Sachna Hanspal, Louise King, Bunmi Oke, Frances Owen,

and Sarah Pocklington, for being just brilliant. Thanks also to my copyeditor Annie Lee, my proofreader Myra Jones, and to my indexer Caroline Wilding for all your help.

To my good friends Alex and Emma at Smith & Gilmour, I can't thank you enough for your beautiful work, for looking at my early sketches and scrapbooks, for being excited when I could barely show you anything, for keeping the faith through ups and downs, and for always knowing that you wanted to design the book.

Huge thanks go to the chefs and contributors – Pete, Ravinder, April, Heston, Guy, Domenica, Caesar, Giuseppe, Gennaro, Danyel, Bella, Rose, Andy, Eddie, Sam, Anna, Sybil, Rachel, Atul, Nigella, Debbie, Jean, Deborah, Kate, Tony, Daniel, Jamie, Adam, Sir Johnny, Ruth, Rosie, Georgie, Alexis, Sarah, Jake, Jody, Alice and Molly – from the 'no longer' to the 'just beginning', and from my family to the world famous, thank you, this book would have been a hell of a lot less yummy without your generous help. To the lovely food stylists – Georgie Socratous, Anna Jones, her assistant Emily Ezekiel, and Sarah Tildesley – all we do, we do together and I thank you. A food photographer is only ever as good as his stylist. To Claire Postans, Jo Lord, Ginny Rolfe, Rebecca Walker, Bethan O'Connor, Louise Holland, Christina Mackenzie and Jodene Jordan from the Jamie team… What would I do without you all?

Finally, thanks go to my dear friends – to Andy Harris, Katie Millard, Nick Pope, Richard Herd, Richard Sinclair, Simon (farmer) Jones, Danyel Couet, Magnus Nygren, Dexter Fletcher, Peter Matthews, Jason Flemyng, John Hamilton, Niall Downing, Peter Hornsey, Ange Morris, Sarah Castleton, Jay Jay and Mel Burridge, Jeffrey Bennett, Peter Matthews, Ruthie and Richard Rogers, Jools Oliver, Charlie Boorman, Rebecca Walker, Tim and Benedict Quick, Sir Johnny and Rosie Scott, Countess Mountbatten, Charlie and Liz Berman, Jeremy King and Guy Botham – thank you for all of your support and for either reading bits and not laughing, or not reading them and avoiding the embarrassment of uncontrolled laughter

To my dearest old friend, the Honourable Timothy Knatchbull, thank you for being my greatest of friends, my biggest supporter, oft my light in a time of darkness, travelling companion and surrogate twin. And to Jamie Oliver, for ignoring the upstarts and the young whippersnappers and sticking with his old buddy, for travelling more miles and spending more time with me than brothers get in a lifetime, for keeping me inspired, for being my constant best mate and for being, with Tim, one of my Musketeers (Hornsey, you can be D'Artagnan), thank you. xx

PERMISSIONS

'Crispy Tempura' reproduced courtesy of Pete Begg. Copyright © Pete Begg 2012; 'Malai Jhingri Poppadoms' reproduced courtesy of Ravinder Bhogal. Copyright © Ravinder Bhogal 2012; 'Oysters Rockefeller' reproduced courtesy of April Bloomfield. Copyright © April Bloomfield 2012; 'Welsh Rarebit or Rabbit à la Heston' reproduced courtesy of Heston Blumenthal. Copyright © Heston Blumenthal 2012; 'Singapore Sling' reproduced courtesy of Guy Botham. Copyright © Guy Botham 2012; 'Lemony Quinoa with Shiitake, Chicken and Coriander' reproduced courtesy of Domenica Catelli. Copyright © Domenica Catelli 2012; 'Bellini Cocktail' reproduced courtesy of Arrigo Cipriani. Copyright © Arrigo Cipriani 2012; 'Gennaro's Pasta and Bean Soup' and 'Gennaro Contaldo's Carpaccio di Branzino con Pompelmo Rosa' reproduced courtesy of Gennaro Contaldo. Copyright © Gennaro Contaldo 2012; 'Conserve de Thon, "Tuna in a Jar"', 'Danyel's Filled Camembert', 'Danyel Couet's Pickles à la Pêche' and 'Pauper's Toast with Chocolate' reproduced courtesy of Danyel Couet. Copyright © Danyel Couet 2012; 'Aromatic Spiced Tea' and 'Aouda's Champagne Cocktail' reproduced courtesy of Bella Crane. Copyright © Bella Crane 2012; 'Focaccia with Black Grapes'; 'Linguine with Broad Beans'; 'Farfalle with Prosciutto, Mint and Peas'; 'Tagliatelle Carbonara with Prosciutto' and 'Zuppa Alla Vongole à la River Café' reproduced courtesy of Rose Gray and Ruth Rogers. Copyright © Rose Gray and Ruth Rogers 2012; 'Egyptian Lentil Soup'; 'Classic Ful Medames'; 'Andaman Island Squid and Pineapple'; 'Chilli Crab'; 'Pomegranate and Red Onion Salad'; 'Grated Cucumber Salad'; 'Cauliflower and Olive Salad'; 'Radish and Orange Salad'; 'Beetroot and Purslane Salad'; 'Herb Salad with Preserved Lemon Dressing'; 'Octopus, Potato and Olive Salad' and 'A Great Starter: "Mixed Poke"' reproduced courtesy of Andy Harris. Copyright © Andy Harris 2012; 'Clams with Sherry and Ham' and 'Mussels Vinaigrette' reproduced courtesy of Eddie Hart and Sam Hart. Copyright © Eddie Hart and Sam Hart 2012; 'Piyajkolir Tarkari: Bengali Prawns', 'Gado Gado' and 'Coconut, Nutmeg and Pistachio Ice Cream Crunch Bombs' reproduced courtesy of Anna Jones. Copyright © Anna Jones 2012; 'Grilled Mackerel with Gooseberry Relish', 'Sybil's Sticky Orange, Kashmiri Chilli and Vodka Cake', 'Sweet Spiced Beef with Green Beans' and 'Papaya and Lime Salsa with Lobster' reproduced courtesy of Sybil Kapoor. Copyright © Sybil Kapoor 2012; 'Wontons in a Smoky Broth' reproduced courtesy of Rachel Khoo. Copyright © Rachel Khoo 2012; 'Nizami Subj Kathi: Spicy Vegetable Wraps' reproduced courtesy of Atul Kochhar. Copyright © Atul Kochhar 2012; 'Overnight Lamb Shanks with Figs and Honey' reproduced courtesy of Nigella Lawson. Copyright © Nigella Lawson 2012; 'Mushroom Ketchup for a Blood-Red Steak'; 'Rhubarb and Gooseberry Charlotte'; 'Una Fragola Surgelata con Cioccolato';

'Apple Timbale with Pine Nuts'; 'Chicken Tagine with Lemon and Olives'; 'Poppy Seed French Toast'; 'Chilled Minted Cucumber and Honeydew Soup'; 'Caesar Salad'; 'Asparagus Vinaigrette'; 'San Francisco Spicy Beets'; 'Marinated Feta with Watermelon, Fennel and Mint'; 'Meatloaf with Relish'; 'Classic Eggs Benedict'; 'Omelette Arnold Bennett' and 'Herrings with Potato à la Suédoise' reproduced courtesy of David Loftus. Copyright © David Loftus 2012; 'Fresh Figs with Hot Espresso Syrup' and 'Date and Coffee Loaf' reproduced courtesy of Debbie Loftus. Copyright © Debbie Loftus 2012; 'Dr Loftus's Sweet and Spicy Tomato Chutney'; 'Masoor Dhal'; 'Blind Date Cookies'; 'Gunning Gingerbread Cookies' and 'Cardamom Fork Cookies' reproduced courtesy of Dr Jean Loftus. Copyright © Dr Loftus 2012; 'Cherry and Almond Cake' reproduced courtesy of Deborah Madison. Copyright © Deborah Madison 2012; 'Mussels in Guinness' reproduced courtesy of Kate McCullough. Copyright © Kate McCullough 2012; 'Wild Rice and Mushroom Soup' and 'Basque Chicken' reproduced courtesy of Tony Milford, Jr. Copyright © Tony Milford, Jr 2012; 'A Welcome from Jamie Oliver'; 'Jamie's Seafood Risotto'; 'Jamie's Italian Marinade for Rabbit'; 'Jamie's Classic Tikka Marinade'; 'Sweet Duck Legs Cooked with Star Anise'; 'Jamie Oliver's Fresh Mackerel Cooked in Pomegranate, Lime Juice and Tequila'; 'Spring and Summer Minestrone'; 'Waldorf Salad Jamie's Way'; 'Mac and Cheese'; 'Jewish Penicillin' and 'Jamie's Kedgeree' reproduced courtesy of Jamie Oliver. Copyright © Jamie Oliver 2012; 'APL's Beef Back Ribs' reproduced courtesy of Adam Perry Lang. Copyright © Adam Perry Lang 2012; 'Victorian Table Manners' reproduced courtesy of Sir Johnny Scott. Copyright © Sir Johnny Scott 2012; 'Scouse Hot Pot' and 'Boti Kebabs' reproduced courtesy of Rosie Scott. Copyright © Rosie Scott 2012; 'Hot Buttered Rum' and 'Spiced Rum Cider' reproduced courtesy of Rosie Scott and Sir Johnny Scott. Copyright © Rosie Scott and Sir Johnny Scott 2012; 'Strawberries and Borage with Flaked Almonds', 'Georgie's Big Greek Tava' and 'Elderflower and Gooseberry Cake' reproduced courtesy of Georgie Socratous. Copyright © Georgie Socratous 2012; 'Fragrant Bengali Fishcakes', 'Tiddly's Chicken Laksa' and 'Coconut, Lime and Mint Granita' reproduced courtesy of Sarah Tildesley. Copyright © Sarah Tildesley 2012; 'Nasi Goreng' reproduced courtesy of Jake Tilson. Copyright © Jake Tilson 2012; 'Vietnamese Spring Rolls' and 'Jody's Green Tea Noodles with Tofu' reproduced courtesy of Jody Vassallo. Copyright © Jody Vassallo 2012; 'Lovage Burgers' and 'Pomegranate and Persimmon Salad' reproduced courtesy of Alice Waters. Copyright © Alice Waters 2012; 'Molly's Apple Pie' and 'Bourbon Pecan Pie' reproduced courtesy of Molly Wrigglesworth. Copyright © Molly Wrigglesworth 2012.

INDEX

SALES BY THE CANDLE.

At GARRAWAY'S COFFEE HOUSE, CORNHILL,
On THURSDAY, September 15, at One precisely,
THE FOLLOWING GOODS, VIZ.
37 Gourds Barbadoes Aloes
30 Chests Gum Arabic   23 Chests Rhubarb
3 Ditto Gum Damar   4 Ditto Cheryeta
30 Ditto Gum Anime   130 Duppers Castor Oil.
Samples will be shewn at No. 3, Clement's-lane, and
Catalogues delivered in due time, by
    BARBER, NEATE, and Co., Brokers,
              3, Clement's-lane.

At No. 10, MINCING-LANE,
On THURSDAY, September 15, at One precisely,
THE FOLLOWING GOODS, VIZ.
150 Chests Havannah Sugar
50 Casks Plantation Coffee
800 Bags Brazil Coffee.
Samples to be seen on the morning of Sale, at No. 10,
Mincing-lane, where Catalogues may be had.
    THOMAS KEMBLE, SON, and Co., Brokers.

At No. 10, MINCING-LANE,
On TUESDAY, September 20, at One precisely,

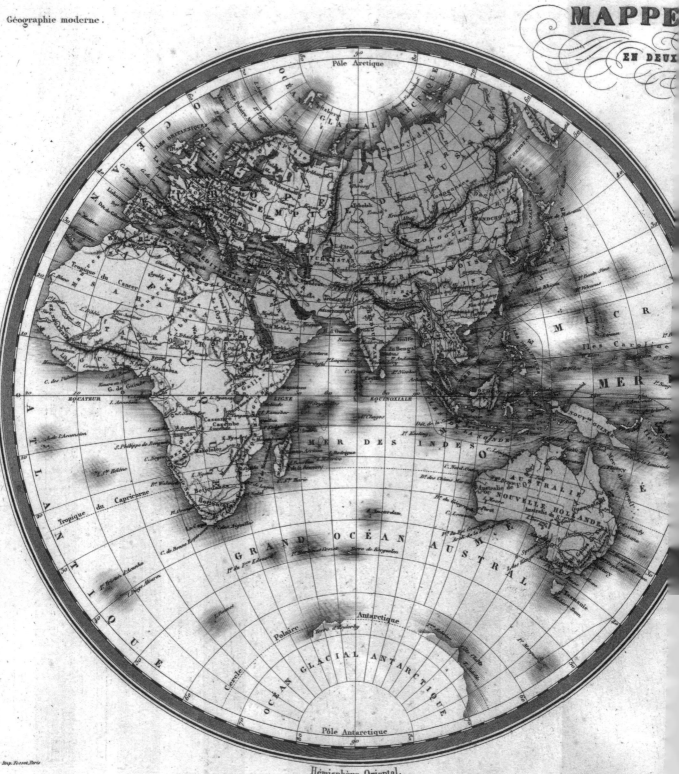

MAPPE

EN DEUX

Imp. Fosset, Paris